The Guardian of Memory

ALDO IZZO AND THE ANCIENT JEWISH CEMETERY OF VENICE

DEDICATION

To Aldo Izzo
a tribute

ISBN: 978-1-910146-83-5 (paperback)
ISBN: 978-1-910146-84-2 (hardback)
Ebooks are available

Published by Solis Press, Lytchett House, 13 Freeland Park, Wareham Road, Poole BH16 6FA, England

Web: www.solispress.com | *Twitter*: @SolisPress

The Guardian of Memory

ALDO IZZO AND THE ANCIENT
JEWISH CEMETERY OF VENICE

MARJORIE AGOSÍN

Photographs by Samuel Shats

Translated by Alison Ridley

Solis Press

Contents

Foreword by Katie Trostel 8

Prologue by Shaul Bassi 10

Aldo Izzo and the Memory of Water 13

The Art of Asking Questions 14

The Pandemic and the Art of Imagining 14

An Ambiguous Cartography 19

The Guardian of Precarious Memory 22

Venice: The Glimpse of Loving Eyes 24

Enchantments and Challenges 25

Venetian Nights 25

Persistent Light Rain on the Lagoon 26

Wind, Sighs, and a Key 27

On the Way to the Lido on a Blue *Vaporetto* 28

The Distant Lido 30

My Notebook of Dreams 30

The Initial Encounter 31

A Man with the Wings of an Angel 34

Entering the Old Jewish Cemetery 34

Strolling Through Wayward Memory 40

Sara Copia Sullam and the Memory of Poetry 44

The Forgotten Women 45

Writing from Behind Closed Gates 46

Sacred and Silent Stones 47

The Angel of Ashes 48

A Farewell Fraught with Uncertainty 50

The Truths of the Pandemic 51

A New Encounter with Aldo 53

Fascism and the Holocaust 54

Aldo, the Voice of History and Memory 57

Leaves of Life and Death 58

The Venetian Jews 59

The Hiding Place During the Shoah 60

Braided Questions 62

The Barges of Death 64

Yom Kippur During the Pandemic 64

Sacred Holidays 65

The Time of the Graceful Sea 66

Living with Absence 67

The Slow Days of the Pandemic 70

Imagined Times During the Confinement 71

The Illusion of Autumns 71

Always Returning to the Lido 74

A Visit to the Dead. 74

The Silence of Permanence 75

Venice and Love 76

Venice and Its Foliage. 77

Returns. 79

The Sounds of Venice. 80

The Imagined City 81

The Opaline Light 84

Footsteps 84

The Ghetto at Nightfall. 86

The Essence of Creativity and Confinement 89

The Ghetto During the Shoah 91

Aldo's House 96

The Bed of Light 97

The Time of Objects .98

A Slow Pace 99

Aldo's Face 101

Pesach in Venice 104

The House of Memory 105

Aldo, Full of Light 107

Of Arrivals and Farewells. 109

Afterword to *The Guardian of Memory*
    by Mark Bernheim 113

The Photographer: Samuel Shats, Ripples in Time ...
    by Mark Bernheim 117

Chronology. 119

Works Cited 123

Acknowledgments 124

A NOTE ON THE TYPEFACES

This book is typeset in Poliphilus which is a facsimile of the font used in *Hypnerotomachia Poliphili*, published by Aldus Manutius in Venice in 1499. Poliphilus replicates fifteenth-century printing on handmade paper—even the original ink spread is reproduced.

Blado, the italic font here was first used by Antonio Blado in 1539.

Foreword by Katie Trostel

Marjorie Agosín's, *The Guardian of Memory*, is a text that embraces liminality. As readers, we are invited to cross its threshold into the life of Aldo Izzo—the steward of the ancient Jewish cemetery of the Lido. His body becomes a port, a harbor, an anchor, and a refuge for stories both personal and collective because, simply put, "Aldo loves memory." His is a fluid biography—a book of memories organized only by the movement of water and shaped by the powerful force of the imagination.

Agosín cares for Aldo's memories and those of his beloved Venetian Jewish community—weaving with words a metaphorical resting place for the past that is always in service of a dynamic future. Within the cartography of poetry, Marjorie and Aldo journey through memory—co-creating meaning as he both metaphorically and literally leads her, arm-and-arm, through the streets of the city. This is a city of porous borders made only of water—a city of thresholds, liminal spaces, and the imagination. She breathes life into scattered stories, stumbling into history—her own footsteps disrupting, and thus activating, the circulation of Jewish memory at once dormant and very much alive.

The accompanying photographic poems by Samuel Shats portray both the grandeur of Venice and its watery canals, but also the intimate scale of memory: the creases of Aldo's face, radiating kindness; his bedroom. Within the folds of this composite story, memory pools and recedes—mirroring the movement of waves as they etch ephemeral patterns on the shoreline.

Composed during the Covid-19 pandemic and its immediate aftermath, the text is a profound meditation on confinement, isolation, and intergenerational trauma—and yet, it insists on the liberatory power of acts of storytelling. Aldo—formerly a ship's captain—steers us through the ebbs and flows of memory, chanting the stories of those whose bodies were confined to ghettoized spaces, but that nevertheless, found freedom in the radically open spaces of the imagination. This guardian of memory is an open poem and Aldo's memory is not stagnant—it flows.

Katie Trostel
Ursuline College, Ohio; coordinator of the
Venice Ghetto Collaboration

Prologue by Shaul Bassi

There is a public story. Once, Jewish monuments were hardly visible in the public domain of Venice, not fully considered as part of the shared cultural heritage of one of the most famous cities in the world. The situation started to change in the 1990s with the restoration of the ancient Jewish cemeteries; ironically, a revival inspired by the dead. Many institutions and individuals contributed to that historic moment, but gradually a man emerged who would come to symbolize the preservation, valorization, and narration of the two cemeteries: Aldo Izzo.

Then there are private stories. A boy, who first experienced death when holding his little dog lifeless in his arms, was consoled by a very elegant man who handed him a piece of paper carrying a prayer for animals. It was also the boy's first encounter with the Jewish tradition of caring for human and non-human creatures. That tender gesture, which has not been forgotten, came from Aldo Izzo.

This year, a middle-aged man has arrived late to the Yom Kippur service at the Levantine Synagogue (the first since the Covid-19 pandemic). At the end of the long day, he hugs a 92-year-old man who has been there for twelve hours: graceful, dignified, unswerving. His shining smile belies the sad events he has endured in his long life, his adamantine optimism always stronger than grief: Aldo Izzo.

I was that boy and now am that middle-aged man; I have witnessed for over thirty years the acts of kindness with which Aldo takes care of the dead and of the living, whether at the side of mourners or as an unrivalled guide for curious visitors.

When Beit Venezia—A Home of Jewish Culture—started its journey in 2009, one of our first projects was titled Jewish childhoods, where we collected the stories of Jews born or living in Venice. Then, as now, we believed that one of the great riches of any community is the lives of its members, in their fascinating diversity. Later we focused on the ways in which Jewish Venice can stimulate the creativity of international artists through a full immersion in its past and present. A major feature of that experience has always been the walk through the cemeteries with Aldo and its evocative stories. It is no coincidence that these walks have inspired multiple artworks, from Hadassah Goldvicht's art project *House of Life*, to the documentary *Aldo's Stones*, where Aldo shares his knowledge with the European Jewish heritage expert Ruth Ellen Gruber. Now Marjorie Agosín's moving poetic meditation adds a fundamental literary chapter to the life and works of this exceptional man.

We owe Marjorie Agosín's presence in Venice to two founders of Beit Venezia, special individuals whose early years (like Aldo's) were marked by the destructive impact of Fascism and Nazism in Europe and who have gifted their intellectual energy to Jewish Venice. American literary scholar Murray Baumgarten's insight that the Ghetto could be reimagined as the international cultural center that it used to be centuries ago was instrumental in the creation of our organization. Napoleone (Leo) Jesurum, a successful manager who retired to Venice to devote himself to the Jewish community of his childhood, shared the same vision. It was Murray's felicitous idea to invite his friend Marjorie to be a writer in residence to honor Leo's memory, an occasion that has also generated new friendships and a wonderful essay.

The Guardian of Memory: Aldo Izzo and the Ancient Jewish Cemetery of Venice brings beautifully together the two mainstays of Beit Venezia, the importance of Jewish Venetian life stories and the role of storytelling for the past, present, and future of the Ghetto. We are extremely grateful to Marjorie Agosín for a new important chapter in the history of Jewish

Venice, and to Samuel Shats, who captures with his poetic images the serene elegance of the stones and water of the city, the serene peace of the cemeteries, and the serene beauty of Aldo's face. And to Aldo, our captain, our warmest wishes to continue, as it is said in the Jewish tradition, *ad me'ah ve'esrimm*, "until 120 years."

Shaul Bassi
Beit Venezia—A Home for Jewish Culture

Aldo Izzo and the Memory of Water

There are certain texts that have no beginning or ending; stories that await patient and curious readers who, in their explorations, fill in the gaps the writer might posit as imagined realities, omissions, or partially composed interludes. Perhaps this story requires, as some literary theorists assert, the arrival of readers who also invent other beginnings and new endings.

This text is a fluid biography, a constellation of fragments about a life filled with adversity and passion. It is fluid like the vertiginous flow of the waters in the city of Venice, in its canals and fountains and archipelagos, in its bridges, in the Bridge of Sighs—the sigh of love as well as death. It is a city made up of little islands that rise and fall during enchanting evenings, each one different from the last, weaving together the memory of those who Aldo Izzo shelters and protects when he buries the dead of Venice's Jewish community and walks along the paths of that city, and especially through the Ghetto, where he appears to be a constant presence.

In wakefulness and in slumber I keep returning to Venice like someone rediscovering an old love. Venice is always becoming, reimagining, and reinventing itself. In order to experience Venice, one has to travel along its canals on its languid and charming *vaporetti* and discover the Adriatic that changes from one moment to the next. I discover Venice at day and at night when I gaze at the sky. Venice is a weightless cloud, a cloud made of stars and stories, as though it is a part of the sky itself.

Within these pages, the reader will encounter Aldo's voice and my voice in a dialogue set to the rhythm of questions and answers, pauses, and syncopes. Each section attempts to recount a time, an instant, an hour—not all at once, but rather intermittently—as though we are engaged in a dance with the words. I invite readers to a rendezvous with memory constructed out of each story, each message sent, each poem, each recollection, all of which—together—represent the remnants of a past that remains before us. I introduce you to Aldo Izzo, the guardian of the Jewish community in Venice, who officiates at all its burials and all of life's ceremonies.

The Art of Asking Questions

Literature, like the ebb and flow of the Adriatic and the Venetian canals, is kinetic like the art of asking questions and receiving answers. It is an intuitive improvisation that happens at unexpected moments. From this back-and-forth of questions and answers, ideas are born, and stories begin to emerge. That is how this story about Aldo was conceived.

I have approached the persona of Aldo Izzo through a dialogue that has its roots in the Talmudic tradition. More than anything, the art of asking questions is the art of perpetuating beauty. Aldo graciously agreed to answer all my inquiries because he is an infinitely generous man. He has made himself available and has poured himself into each and every response. And although Aldo always talks about absences, everything in him resonates presence.

This text reflects my fluid conversations with Aldo from 2019 until the present. We met for the first time in person in Venice in 2019. Then we remained in contact throughout the worst part of the pandemic by way of email correspondence. Finally, in spring of 2022, I was able to return to Venice to see him again. Throughout this span of time, the questions and answers have continued to flow.

The Pandemic and the Art of Imagining

While the pandemic cut some lives short, it repaired others who were able to find themselves during that time. Covid necessitated a new way of communicating and new ways of being creative. This compilation of texts (letters, poems, reflections) is one of the results. The collection, which can be read sporadically, is, more than anything, a love story about getting to know oneself and others in spite of absences and distances.

For me, the pandemic became a way of reimagining the world. I recognized that the world as we knew it was gone forever, that we would have to find new ways of living in a world we were witnessing fade away. The epistolary experience allowed me to get to know another human being

by way of letters that seemed to have their own inner dialogue. The relationship that grew between Aldo and me was, perhaps, the greatest gift I received during the pandemic. Aldo's company was central to me finding myself anew, to feeling the love of one human being for another. I felt as though everything was returning in a different way. Nature emerged in all its majesty, as did literature, creativity, and humanity (in its ability to face challenges).

The majority of this book—or lyrical rendering of a life—originates from a period of unprecedented solitude for humanity, but also, a time of infinite possibilities for change. As mentioned above, I began my email correspondence with Aldo during the pandemic and, after receiving his first brief message, our communication over time transformed into a conversation made up of infinite meanings, as many as the numerous canals that surround Venice and the space inhabited by Aldo. I felt I could relate to each message, each letter, each experience with Aldo. Sometimes, for example, when Aldo would write about his childhood in Venice, it would bring back memories of my own childhood in Chile.

I wanted to write about Aldo in a way that someone might recount a story about a lost love or like a message in a bottle that makes its way to the Adriatic. However, more than anything, I wanted to write about the purity and dignity of his soul, his dedication to burying the dead in his community, and the gratifying honor of knowing him and learning from his commitment. And, when all was said and done, our discourse allowed me to get to know myself better and understand the reason why I decided to dedicate myself to this project that has been a new adventure in my writing.

Writing the World
In the restless hours
When twilight yields its hours
To the great night of the world,
When longing and stillness drift
In the ambiguity of every evening,
It is then, in the hour of dislocated times
And in the hour when the spirits of memory return,
That you retreat to the forest path.

The path and the tortuous fog are your guides.
You walk with the slowness of the violet hour.
The dead watch over you,
And you arrive at a portal where a light pulsates
In the heart of the night of the world.
You are guided by that light ...

A mahogany table awaits you,
A notebook brimming with autumns
And a blank page.
You write and you begin
In the solitude of the night.
The dream of poetry emerges,
The blue rose,
Its wilted petals,
Because they have died
And want to live again.

You awake amid words.
Everything in you grows.
Your fingers are seeds.
They embroider words.
You have arrived ...
On the invisible table
You write the world.

It seems that creativity flourishes in moments of great solitude. It is important to remember that one of the first countries affected by the virus was Aldo Izzo's Italy, a country where art abounds, where life is shaped by music, sculptures, and fallen angels. And therefore, it should not surprise us that, early on in Italy, people began to sing from their balconies in order to communicate with one another and spread solidarity, beauty, and love.

An Ambiguous Cartography

What the reader will find in this meditation is my composite perception of Aldo, a beloved—and sometimes contested—figure drawn from multiple questions and answers, conversations that attempted to synthesize his daily life and his comings and goings in and around the world. It is a text that also attempts to tell the story of his experience as a Jew in a community that is dwindling, as well as his experiences during Jewish holidays, moments that Aldo tells me he used to celebrate with his wife, his daughters, and his grandchildren. Now, for the most part, he spends those occasions alone, remembering loved ones who are no longer with him in person, while gazing out from the large terrace of his home that faces the Lido.

I must say that Aldo is one of the few people I know who lives for truth and justice. He tries, more than anything, to do good. He is also an individual who behaves ethically in every step he takes in life; steps which paradoxically are the same ones that lead us closer to the mystery of death. In our conversations, Aldo explains that he is certain of nothing, and that in spite of all that uncertainty, what he values most are the Jewish traditions.

Aldo Izzo's life's story starts with him as a Venetian Jewish child and then as an adult, a lover of education and reading, who, over the years, learned a number of languages, because in his home many were spoken. On one occasion, I asked him about his multilingual abilities and he answered:

> *How many languages do I know? Italian, English, Spanish. I also used to speak French and could write it well too, but it has been a long time since I used it. I'm out of practice … And, if you don't use a*

language, you lose it. However, I read it without difficulty. I know a bit of Croatian and some (very little) of other languages, thanks to my profession for thirty years …

Aldo's profession as a ship's captain not only brought him close to the sea and its mysteries, but also to faraway destinations where he learned to interpret human nature.

This is the story I am attempting to tell from a distance. I am building memory by way of what is said and what is left unsaid, by way of words

that refer to a time of cruelty, replete with both neglect and dreams, much like Aldo's story in a city of resplendent beauty that comes and goes, that flows and returns like the indecipherable mystery of its waters, like life portrayed at dawn or the smile of someone who tries to repair the world by safeguarding forgotten experiences.

This book can be read like an obscure map with brief interludes of light. It is an ambiguous cartography, like the waters of Venice exhibiting sparkles of light that disappear into infinity as though they never existed. Each vignette is a fragile thread that reflects Aldo's experience in the world as captured in his silences, in what he forgets and writes on napkins or in old notebooks, and in fragments of a storm and its shadows; fragments of light braided together in visions of a Venice that remains intact despite the passing centuries.

Without a doubt, this conversation is a great love letter to life and to the conscious and subconscious universe motivated by Aldo's experiences; a love letter written over a year-and-a-half during a time when the Covid pandemic made us question human nature and our fragile ambitions that had been cut short by an invisible enemy. At the same time, we also began to reimagine ourselves and to ponder our past and our new future.

The Guardian of Precarious Memory

I believe that, behind the art of words—Aldo's in particular—there is an underlying energy, a force that later produces a myriad of emotions, profound images that mere translation into writing could never convey. As a result of our conversations and my time in Venice, I feel that everything related to the Venetian experience belongs to a hidden alphabet, an order where signs allude to clues or half-open doors, mysterious windows that make one ponder who might have lived in those golden palaces. Could it be the shadow of the dead who appear like guests at a festive gathering of ghosts? Venice is one of those cities where beings appear and disappear, where recollections emerge like a halo of living memory evolving through the canals of time above a city that since long ago has been a place for merchants, nomads, and poets. Aldo Izzo and Venice are inseparable. They are a being and a city that travel between spaces in time through doorways and mirrors; they are from here and from the hereafter. That is who Aldo Izzo is: the guardian of memory.

Thanks to my conversations and epistolary encounters with Aldo, I understood the importance of safeguarding the memory of the dead and a culture this is continually shrinking, without expecting anything in return. Individuals who selflessly care for the dead and for those who visit them are the noblest of human beings.

Venice: The Glimpse of Loving Eyes

I met Aldo Izzo for the first time in June 2019 thanks to an invitation from the Jewish Venetian community and Beit Venezia to serve as a visiting writer. The invitation was extended by two academics: Murray Baumgarten and Shaul Bassi. I was very excited and I accepted immediately, motivated primarily by an idea I had been pondering for some time. I wanted to visit and write about the Jewish cemetery in the Lido as well as the closed space of the Ghetto as a place of creativity and openness. I wanted to understand how forced confinement could lead to the production of literary works. And, although no one episode is ever completely like another, later when I began to write this book, the isolation of the Ghetto reminded me of the isolation of the pandemic in 2020, the forced confinement caused by a virus.

That is how I arrived in Venice during an unusually cold May, which surprised me since that time of year is ordinarily referred to as the month of blossoms. It is a month filled with afternoons that further illuminate the history of a city that, although sinking, nevertheless emerges in the imagination as a constant presence for those who write about it.

During the months of my stay, I tried to live, feel, and smell the city in all its splendor, observing each detail so nothing would escape my notice. It was a task that I apparently took very seriously as I was frequently restless and had trouble sleeping. I wanted to write something distinctive, something different from what other poets had already written about this city. I didn't want to imitate anyone; I was looking for my own voice. Something in me wanted to remain alert all day and all night in order to hear what the Venetians refer to as the *acqua alta*.

Enchantments and Challenges

I was eager to walk down every path, travel along every canal, touch every stone of the ancient walls that from midnight to dawn once enclosed other lives like mine. The city emits a mysterious sound that always seems to suggest a submerged presence while the *vaporetti*'s horns and the bells of San Moisè's Church (which is close to where my husband and I were staying in a building with no tenants except for us) sound out through the sacred night. In my observations, I sensed that Venice was handing me its keys, like Aldo would soon hand me the keys to the Beit Chaim cemetery where he would be waiting for me the next day by the ancient door while our dead watched on. As I imagined him opening the cemetery gate, I thought about the significance of his work.

Venetian Nights

In Venice, no night is the same as another. To walk around this city is to live in wonder and to conjure up footsteps of travelers who may have emerged from palaces cloaked in shadow or from the hereafter, from the faraway realm of death. Venice is an opaline city where everyone appears to travel in a time outside of time, and every mirror is a gateway between the here and now and what once was. Venice is a city that suddenly fades away only to reemerge like a dream bathed in water. Venice bewitches and enchants those who are not afraid to look deeply into its essence.

And even though Venetian nights are dark and deep, they imbue us with a certain clarity that allows us to process what we experience during the light of day. At night, the palaces are in full splendor, illuminated by a faint light that hints at a presence that is no longer there. At night, everything is an illusion.

Persistent Light Rain on the Lagoon

I am remembering a night during my visit when the north and south sea winds converge while I listen to the lament of the water and the *vaporetti*, the charming boats that transport tourists who are in awe of the city's magnificence. Might those precarious and ageless boats be the remnants of ancient times, as though the past is returning to us? The rain falls on this kingdom of night. I look out the window to find no one there, and yet I envision everyone in this city of water where imagination and memory unite. What I dreamed last night is interrupted by today's dreams. The bells of San Moisè's Church chime as though they beckon from the distance of a memory where the rain submerges us in prophecies. That is how Venice fills me with questions even though I am not searching for answers. I ask myself if the rain in this city might have its own unique spirit or if it might be different from the rain that falls outside my window. I delve once more into the hollowness of sleep where the texture of this night attends to my words and I fall asleep to its cadence. I am free while I listen to the light rain on the lagoon.

Wind, Sighs, and a Key

In order to enter improbable cities like Venice, one needs to dream and remember the Bridge of Sighs that connects the passage between day and night and the rhythms of the water that whispers. One must stop and listen to the language of the wind and the water. There would be no Venice without the wind, just as there would be no Venice without sighs. And yet, in order to enter, someone must give you the key: the key to life and death, the key to boats and canals, the key to travel and time.

To get around in this labyrinthine city that has no precise addresses, one must open many doors. However, some will remain closed forever, perhaps eaten away by the vicissitudes of a history that emerges only later in literature. I have faith in my patience and in the power of literature to help me understand this nocturnal place with its facades and canals, this city watched over by the figure of Aldo Izzo.

And so, I wake in this city that welcomes me, that invites me to return to it time and time again, that makes me feel alive like the water that flows through my senses; a living water that draws me closer to love and obeisance, to the signs drawn by its canals.

I must go to meet with Aldo Izzo ... While I think about the other commitments I have in the city, I remember I have to meet a journalist this morning who wants to interview me about my life as an author and my visit to Venice. She is running late, because in this city it seems that there are no clocks, that we return to the time of love and beauty, to the time of Venice and its canals.

When the journalist arrives at last, I also take my time answering her questions, thereby adapting to the rhythm of the city and its water. The journalist seems to know more about my life than I do. I listen to her talk about my memories as though she is speaking about a painting in which I am one of its subjects building the memory of this city.

On the Way to the Lido on a Blue Vaporetto

Suddenly, Shaul Bassi, my host, knocks on the old window of the café by the Piazza San Marco where I am sitting with the journalist. I see him hurriedly enter and I remember that in Venice both those who are in a hurry and those who take their time are all traveling on the same path, the same canal boat. I would like to play with the unique sense of time in this city, to dance with it and be its light and darkness at the same time, but Shaul wakes me from my reverie with that tone of voice of his that is somewhere between distant and endearing. "Marjorie, you are going to be late getting to the Lido, and Aldo won't be able to wait for you, because it may well rain, and I don't want Aldo to have to wait for you in the rain." I bid the journalist farewell as she continues speaking about my life as a young adult. I see out of the corner of my eye that she has raised her hand as though asking for an explanation as I walk away. I run for the *vaporetto* that will take me to the Lido as tourists from all over the world, along with street vendors, make me falter.

THE GUARDIAN OF MEMORY: ALDO IZZO

I see the Doge's Palace and I can already sense a new type of happiness washing over me; something is going to change my life and my understanding of memory and my work on that subject. I sense it is the happiness of a reunion with the experiences of a people, the Jewish people, lost within the walls of this city. They are my people who, despite the injustices of history, continue to prevail. I think about that a lot on the *vaporetto* because I am finally going to meet Aldo who takes care of the memories of the Jewish people in Venice and anywhere else where the laws of the Torah are followed.

The Distant Lido

The Lido seems like an island far away from Venice, but that might just be an optical illusion. Everything in Venice is a mirror of what it once was and what it could have been, or what it is not. I like traveling to the Lido on the *vaporetto* full of people and seeing how they get off at different stops that have names in a language that sounds like it is sung and makes one fall in love: Salute, Accademia, Giardini ... Each stop could be a poem or the greatest of adventures to imagine. Each stop is remembered over and over again and always in a different way.

My Notebook of Dreams

As I make my way to the Lido on the *vaporetto*, I jot in my notebook:

> *When one looks at Venice, it is always like seeing it for the first time ...*

I feel as though I am learning about birth and death in this city. I write down the words for "to give birth" in Italian: "*dare alla luce.*" Being on the water in Venice feels to me like being born again, like coming into the light, a different kind of light.

I stop writing to look at the Basilica di Santa Maria della Salute, which is simply majestic. Like poetry, everything in Venice has the rhythm of abundance or that beauty that hides in the most sacred part of the soul. Small Venice, submerged Venice, beautiful Venice, vulnerable Venice.

I return to my journal and write:

> *Venice is like a fine rain, like the caresses of a distant yet present love ... The Lido is at the end of the lagoon like a sunset or the texture of nostalgia, a sunset to remember all that eludes us. And the memory of this city, that is as ephemeral as it is elusive, represents a wing of the wind that seeks refuge between the stones ...*

I close my notebook, because we have finally arrived at the Lido. A taxi awaits to take us to the Jewish cemetery.

The Initial Encounter

I am apprehensive about this encounter, because I do not know Aldo and I have never visited these tombs that represent the ancestral memories of the Jewish people. They are a people who history has always sought to destroy and bury, a people who at one time (like so many others) lived

confined within ghettos, listening every night to the creak of a door latch that signaled the internment of experience and life behind enormous gates. Here, in Venice, echoes of distant sobs can still be heard in the water that runs through it. And I hear those same sobs in my heart ... However, today there is a beautiful sun that illuminates the figure of Aldo Izzo who is waiting for me at the gates of the Beit Chaim Cemetery. Aldo, the keeper of keys, the custodian of the living and the dead, greets me with his aqueous gaze as he leans his ancient bicycle against a wooden door.

The Winged Bicycle

Aldo Izzo travels on his winged bicycle
As though in one of Chagall's dreams
Where the world flies and smiles
And ancestral stones sing.

Aldo approaches serenely.
He unwaveringly opens the gates
To the ancient Jewish cemetery in the Lido.
In this instant when the calendar
Goes back centuries,
The silence of the dead reaches us.
They await us,
They invite us to enter.

The doors open,
And in the distance cats purr.
The sun settles on the tombs
And on Aldo's face
That is a map weathered
By light and shadows ...

The bicycle rests and dreams.
It has folded its wings.
In the distance the sea also awaits.
Everything awaits ...

The tombs lean and bow to us ever so slightly
In a prodigious tangle between death and life.
Aldo chants and tells stories.
From his lips emerges the light of God,
The challenges of faith.

A Man with the Wings of an Angel

Aldo Izzo is such a tall man that when he embraces you it seems his hands encircle your head, as though a fallen angel is greeting you, welcoming you not at the doors to heaven, but rather those to Earth ...

On this first encounter, I ask him, "When did you decide to look after this cemetery with such care? Why do you do it, Aldo?" He answers that it is what he is supposed to do, and I understand at that moment that Aldo's responsibility stems from his commitment to Judaism and the history of its people. He explains: "More than a religious responsibility, I prefer to think of it as a responsibility to our persecuted people ..." At least that's what he declares when he admits that he does not pray every day, but that he always celebrates Shabbat.

In some ways, Aldo is the person who initiated the renovation of the Jewish cemetery. I thought the Lido cemetery was the oldest in Europe, but Aldo corrects me:

> Remember, Marjorie, it is not the oldest in Europe as you say. Our cemetery in the Lido came into existence in 1386. The one in Worms on the shores of the Rhine in Germany originated in 1100, and I believe the one in Prague is more recent; it emerged around 1478
> ...

I ask myself what it must be like to care for the dead, to keep them company, and to preserve the memory of the living ...

Entering the Old Jewish Cemetery

The cemetery keys, although large, seem to weigh nothing at all. Could it be they too have wings? They are like the angels that perch atop the leaning tombs. It feels as though everything here is light like the wind and its sighs.

ENTERING THE OLD JEWISH CEMETERY

Aldo's Keys
Aldo's keys
Sound like a bell,
Or sometimes like the high tide
Of Venetian hours,
And at night they rest
On a wall made of noble wood.

Aldo's keys
That cross thresholds,
That open doorways,
Gates that slide
Between ancestries.

Only Aldo carries them.
With determination and elegance
He opens the gate to the cemetery
With a gentle cadence,
And soon the wind of God
Enters through the walls.

THE GUARDIAN OF MEMORY: ALDO IZZO

In the Lido, one always senses that the water is nearby because of its smells and its sounds, even though it is out of sight. The tombs in the oldest part of the cemetery date from the fourteenth century.[1] They still have Hebrew inscriptions and, among the tangle of weeds and fallen trees from recent storms, one can sense the passage of time, the centuries of history of the Jewish people. I think about all these names. These people lived in the Venetian Ghetto and loved both the light and the dark. The dark was the measure of days while the light was the measure of unerring nights, the time of confinement.

Enlightenment happened when night arrived, and the gates were locked. Nights were filled with possibilities. Books were published, people gathered, and women sang. Some audacious ones also wrote. At this moment, I feel like I am walking with Aldo through the house of life, a life where one enters and perceives the proximity of the tree of memory. Each name is a leaf replete with memories.

As a child, I was never afraid of cemeteries like my friends were. I think I loved the tranquility of those places, the silence of words that rest on tombstones cloaked in leaves that fall; leaves like necklaces embroidered

---

1 This footnote and the ones that follow were written by a former student of mine, Bethany Pasko. Bethany also penned the chronology at the end of this book. I thank Bethany for the careful research she did for me on the old cemetery at the Lido and the Venetian Ghetto. Here, Bethany recounts the origins of the cemetery: At the advent of the fourteenth century, the Lido cemetery was formed, serving as a permanent site to commemorate the dead of the Jewish community in the Venetian Ghetto. In 1386, the doge offered for the Jews to purchase a piece of land, a parcel that could be used as a cemetery. The Piovego handled the transaction, which was met with notable backlash, as the religious community located in San Nicolò did not want to relinquish the land (Calimani, p. 9). The land itself was relatively thin, acting as a geographic barrier between the Venetian lagoon and the Adriatic Sea (*World Monuments Fund*). The refusal of the group to cede the land is emblematic of the antisemitism that permeated every aspect of Venetian society. A lawsuit followed, with the group suing the Venetian magistracy, but finally, an agreement was reached in 1380 (Calimani, p. 9).

in the stone. I enter the House of Life on Aldo's arm. Even though he is in his nineties, he exudes great physical and, above all, spiritual strength, just as this cemetery does. Despite its historical significance, it is a place that is small, like a house with hidden windows that safeguards the history of those who once lived in Venice, leaned out their windows, and sang in low voices at dawn, or perhaps prayed and gave thanks.

The Dead Appear at Dinner Time
Amid the stillness of tranquil things
You learn and you move closer to them …
They have come from a land that is far away,
But is known to all.
They cross doorways, thresholds, the time of solitude.
They reach you as though they are waiting for you,
And you for them …

Their journey is porous.
They cross borders, rivers …
They are silent travelers in an infinite geography.
At first, the light attempts to accompany them,
But they need silence and a stirring darkness,
Where light settles like a nest, a refuge,
A moment between coming and going …

They arrive at your table
Where you've saved their favorite seats,
Prepared their favorite foods.
They say they've come for only a few short minutes,
Those minutes are years or maybe centuries …
They tell you they've always been with you,
Especially at twilight
When the forests become enchanted,
When the fairy-tale deer
Move slowly among the ferns,
When the fog is clad in its rain-drenched robes.
They are also made of water and rain …

They tell you they like the wind, the bearer of messages,
The wind that praises the words of the living,
That prays for them, the dead.

They are present for an instant,
Or it might be a century.
Do you recognize them?
Do you hear their lithe footsteps,
Like the gaze of God upon the fields?
It's them, you whisper. It's them,
The ones you always awaited
Like one awaits a dream.
They come in silence so as not to disturb you.
Surreptitiously, they light candles.
Mirrors begin to glow,
They ignite the distant lantern of love.

You might imagine they have come for a fete,
But they wear neither clothes nor shoes.
Even though you can always make out their footsteps,
Steps amid the shadow of water,
You are surprised before a presence that nothing can evade.
But the knowledge of that presence
Dwells in what remains unsaid.
You will learn that silence merges
With unspoken words.
You will learn that at the hour of your death
An angel will return to close your eyes.
That darkness is also another kind of light.
Someone opens a window, a door, a gate …

Your guests have departed.
They await you in a distant landscape
That ambles through the mist.
You were not able to bid them farewell,
But you will see them again someday or every day.
Your dead have returned.
You awake bathed in golden light.

Strolling Through Wayward Memory

Aldo walks ahead of me like a guardian angel showing the way. With each of his slow and measured steps, he illuminates the path before us. He has been walking through this cemetery for more than eighty years. Even so, I feel as though this outing—the one he is taking with me today and those he has taken with other visitors on a regular basis—brings him the same joy as the first. Aldo walks among the tombs with the slowness of those who respect memory, with the parsimony of someone who does not want to disturb the dead for whom he cares while, from time to time, he bids them good morning or good evening.

My feet sink into the narrow path that spans the cemetery, a path covered in dry leaves that dream about returning in spring, leaves that love to dress the tombs in a green hue that symbolizes life.

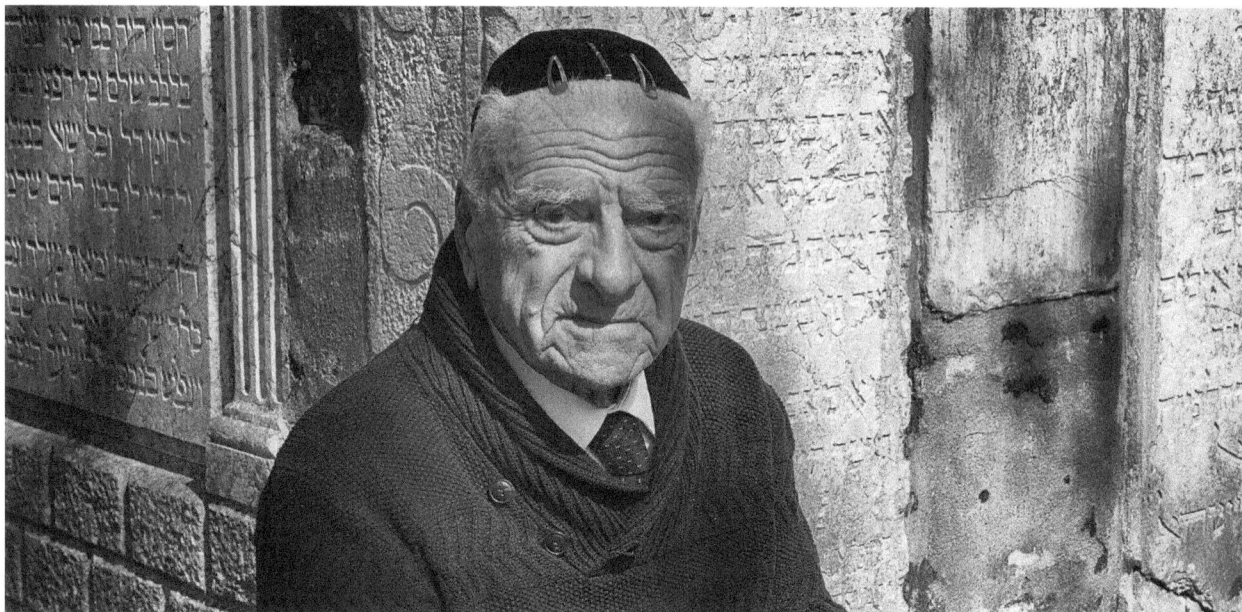

THE GUARDIAN OF MEMORY: ALDO IZZO

In this part of the cemetery, the tombs have inscriptions in Ladino, Italian, Spanish, Portuguese, and Hebrew.[2] I stop before each one and try to reconstruct a story that, even on stone, is being erased. It is difficult to read the inscriptions, but Aldo knows them all by heart. He reads them out loud to me. I feel as though I am delving into the memory of my people in Beit Chaim. Here death has not erased their tombstones and even less their lives, because Aldo Izzo, who in my eyes is an angel, sheds light on them and keeps them company.

Sara Copia Sullam and the Memory of Poetry

And so, I arrive at Sara Copia Sullam's tomb. I have read about her, but I want to know more. I want to think about each of these people as though they still travel on the city's canals. I ask myself who they were and what they did, what they wrote and what they dreamed. I stop before an old stone bench. As I rest, the air fills with the sweetest silence in which I can make out the sound of the sea, the sound of the wind, the sound of life that moves among these tombs and tell stories. Suddenly I think there can be no death as long as memory exists and someone writes about their experiences as they stroll through this Venice marked by its bridges and the breath of the water with its soft emergent swells. And I think that perhaps all its bridges could be the Bridge of Sighs, perhaps they are nothing more than minor and transitory paths that connect that space to ours. Perhaps each bridge is a return, a farewell …

I ask Aldo if we can move a little closer to Sara Copia Sullam's tomb. She was a Venetian poet who lived in the city's Ghetto, in that enclosed space where at night guards locked all the Jews behind enormous gates.

---

2 The multilingual inscriptions further intensify the feelings of displacement and the conglomeration of identities that fully formed in the Venetian Ghetto.

The history of the Jews is always the same. They are always ostracized and always confined. They are destined to live like Sara who wrote from within that enclosed space and who, at night, could be heard singing when she opened her small window to let in the sound of the water.

Sara represents the proud and noble presence of a woman who resided in the Venetian Ghetto. She wrote and sang in several languages: Italian, Hebrew, and sometimes Greek. She also hosted gatherings in her house for important people associated with the fine arts. We do not know much about her, but some say she was stunningly beautiful, while others say she provided financial assistance to ship owners in exchange for them giving her lessons and teaching her the things she wanted to learn. Sara wanted to achieve a higher level of education than that to which women had access at the time.

Sara was an essential part of the Ghetto. She lived there, loved there, created there, and was also betrayed there by those who were supposedly her friends. Out of jealousy, or perhaps insecurity in the presence of Sara's brilliant mind, certain men plotted to humiliate and silence her. Nevertheless, despite the betrayals, Sara's name continues to transcend the walls of the Ghetto and she exists in a space beyond borders.

The Forgotten Women

As I gaze at her tomb, I remember her and the other women who have been forgotten. I think about those who no one speaks about and those who have achieved great feats without asking for any kind of recognition. I think about the women who have been betrayed, like Sara, or who may have been the objects of malicious comments or judgments rife with superstition and ignorance. One does not need to be particularly astute to realize that women have always been at the forefront of being the victims of discrimination. In the history of this city, Jewish women were associated with prostitution, moral decadence, plague, and capriciousness. Perhaps in the case of the Jewish women in the Ghetto, they were singled out because they aroused the curiosity of those who saw in their beauty a strange and seductive force that had to be confined and made invisible.

Writing from Behind Closed Gates

Sara recited and sang, and, although she could not travel literally, she traveled figuratively. Even in death her voyage continues because memory neither stagnates nor stops. Memory flows like these canals or like an anecdote that changes through the years, the same way we change as we pass through these basins. Every journey brings us closer to death where, in stillness, one remembers, just as we remember the figure of Sara gazing out at the wind and the lagoon.

Up until now, Sara's story was not particularly clear to me, as no one knew precisely where she died or where she was buried. However, happily for me, I found her in this place, in the perpetual silence of death. How difficult it must have been to feel the words so deeply, to write about the desire for freedom. How difficult it must have been to be confined within the Ghetto when one understands the echo of words, when it is possible to hear them. How difficult it must have been to write those words at midnight and read them aloud. In my imagination, I take out a slim book of Sara's poems and begin to read. The wind comes in off the lagoon and with it, distant stories. A small leaf lands on my hands and I imagine it is Sara who has returned.

Sacred and Silent Stones

Today, in honor of Sara and all the other forgotten women, I pick up a few colored stones.[3] "This stone is for you, Sara, my friend. This stone that bathed in the canals' waters, that knows about countless journeys, comings and goings, including your own, will keep the memory of your work alive and the works of so many others that have been lost. I leave this stone here to watch over you and to contribute to the long sought-after refuge where other men and women like you can hide from terror. It will be a refuge against fear and betrayal."

I will have to return many times to reunite with Sara since the dead await us so that others might hear their voices. Aldo stops in front of Sara's grave and tells me that he loves all the tombs equally, that he cares for them with his life.

> **The Old Cemetery**
> I approach so as not to wake them, the dead,
> Those who love the permanence of hours,
> Hours that will turn into centuries,
> Or perhaps just seconds
> When an evanescent memory finds them.
>
> Thousand-year-old foliage shrouds me,
> The stones await me where every silence speaks.
> I enter without haste.
> The tangle of trees shelters my steps.
> I enter centuries,
> I traverse them unhurriedly.

---

3 The lasting nature of the stones perhaps further symbolizes this community, steadfast in their faith, devoted in both life and in death. Through paying respects, one does not only acknowledge contributions through life, but also the fortitude that came through the seemingly simple day-to-day act of living one's Jewish faith.

I am sun and water,
Memory and stone.

I read the faded names,
I feel them too ... They are here.
They await us.
They know how to wait.
The leaning tombs ask to be caressed.
I am here, devoted to these crossroads,
To the ephemeral distance
Between life and death.

Suddenly the cats in Venice begin to mew.
Everything is a weave of stories,
A murmur of voices,
A whisper.
Perhaps they are angels
Who safeguard my steps
And the sacred shadows
Of the house of life.

The Angel of Ashes

In this city, Aldo is not only the caretaker of cemeteries, but also the guardian of Venetian Jewish culture, and most, if not all, of the people who live here benevolently call him the Angel of Ashes. I think the ashes that still hover over our memory belong to those whose lives ended in Auschwitz. All of Europe might be a field of ashes. They say that the local rabbi does not allow those who have been cremated to be buried, so it is Aldo who prays for them and sings in silence so that all who arrive at his cemetery find peace. Aldo welcomes everyone with his sailor's hat in hand and a smile that lights up both the living and the dead. Aldo Izzo, the Angel of Ashes that are rekindled in the darkness of night.

The Angel of Ashes
The hour approaches …
We have been awaiting it ever since we learned
The art of being born and the art of living.
It is that hour that is perhaps violet
Or the color of an errant light.

You recently came to recognize that,
Despite its unpredictability,
Its fragility and its joy,
The world delights you,
But you know you will travel to a different land,
The one that is on the other shore of the sea
Far to the north,
The sea of ashes …

Nothing and everything awaits you.
Someone will gift you a cluster of lights and grapes.
You will forget the geography of your body,
But not the sensation of how much you loved while inhabiting it.
You will see the faces of your parents
Who in all the dark places have watched over you,
And you will adapt to the stillness,
To the silent repose and the hours beyond hours,
Like the hours before birth …

The angels of ash await you,
The angels of intermittent memory,
Of life that obscures nothing,
Of death that knows everything and is a faithful friend.
Around you the wind and the wings of angels
With their infinite faces,
With the incantatory light of their gazes.

A Farewell Fraught with Uncertainty

I say goodbye to Aldo with a sadness that's caused by the uncertainty of not knowing if I will see him again. Will he tell me other stories about the cemetery, about those he looks after so painstakingly in this place? Will he tell me the story of those who for centuries have rested here, and who are now under his care? I think when I return to Venice, the rain will not be the same and neither will its people who look furtively at the ancient windows of the *palazzi*.

During my trip I learned the importance of empathy, of not fearing the solitude of days and nights, and I also learned that the act of looking after a cemetery is to safeguard the memory of a culture. In fact, Aldo,

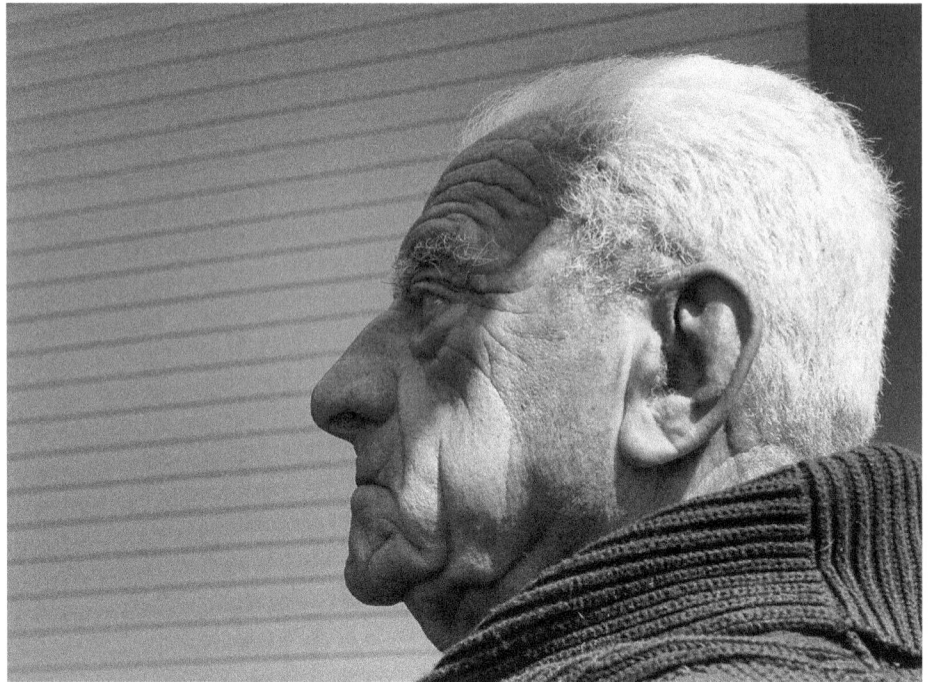

the Angel of Ashes, is, to me, the angel of our memory, and when I recall our walks through the galleries of the cemetery, I always remember the generous smile of the helmsman who leads—without asking for or receiving anything in return—what remains of a community that is continually drifting away across the great Lido lagoon.

The Truths of the Pandemic

After my trip in 2019, I didn't hear from Aldo for several months. It comforted me to think about his eyes filled with light despite having seen death up close so many times. The image of Aldo waiting for us at the entrance of the cemetery became vitally important to me. I kept going back to it as one returns to Venice in dreams.

In March of 2020, the Covid pandemic assaulted the world with a cruelty we had not experienced since the Spanish flu of 1918–1920. Covid-19 became a type of plague that laid bare all the material inequities that we still, despite all our technological advances, have been unable to eradicate. Poverty and hunger were apparent to everyone on the planet, and we were filled with doubt and uncertainty during the lockdowns. Our way of relating to others also changed, as did our feelings, and language itself.

Despite the uncertainty created by the virus, there were certain things that may have benefited from the time of confinement. For example, Venice returned to its postcard image of itself as the clouds above the Adriatic returned to the great lagoon. While social media claimed that the swans and dolphins returned to the canals, that was not true. However, the absence of boat activity made the water much clearer.

During the time of confinement, people sought refuge in books and perhaps many of us searched for the innermost parts of our souls. That time marked a new way of living in the world, of rethinking and reimagining it. For a writer, living in imaginative solitude is familiar. Nevertheless, the impossibility of having direct contact with the world affected us all.

During the lockdown, I thought a lot about loved ones all over the world, especially those who were so far away. We were all united in the face of pain and anxiety. Then I thought about Aldo, and I wanted to write to him to find out how he was. Despite the physical distance between us, I always returned to Venice to speak with him, to that ineffable Venice that comes and goes amid memories and that draws ever closer in my mind. As I think about the confinement again, it's hard for me to imagine Venice behind closed doors, because, in my experience, imagination soars freely in that city.

At the beginning, my communication with Aldo consisted only of brief emails. Then, as our correspondence became more intimate and more frequent, I got up the courage to ask him if I could write a book about him. He agreed and has been very enthusiastic about the project ever since. He often asks me about its progress:

> My dearest Marjorie, Shabbat shalom! I am very happy that the book is progressing and that you are writing it with such dedication, passion, and love. I dream about the day when I will have it in my hands …

I am not sure this book would have come to fruition in the way that it has, had it not been for the pandemic. Of course, it would have been easier to go to Venice with a tape recorder and ask Aldo questions directly, but the flow of time during the pandemic allowed me to envision and create this multifaceted text that contemplates a life dedicated to the common good, a life full of subtleties and complexities. The pandemic taught me that, in times of extreme isolation, creativity can flourish, just as it did in the past in the Venetian Ghetto.

THE GUARDIAN OF MEMORY: ALDO IZZO

A New Encounter with Aldo

It was thanks to my correspondence with Aldo during the pandemic that I began to know him better. His biography became clearer to me as we wrote to each other nearly every day and I could ask him all the questions that had occurred to me since we met in person in 2019.

Aldo told me that he was born in Venice on August 28, 1930. His mother was Jewish, but his father was not. He said he had a brother, Alberto, but didn't say much more than that he enjoyed playing with him. Sometimes I feel like Aldo's narration breaks off, perhaps because words are incapable of expressing so much suffering. I think I might be delving into forgotten territories that my friend has tried to leave behind. It is as though Aldo sometimes wants to disappear for a second from the horizon recreated by my questions. He wrote to me once:

> It is good to remember beautiful things like you do. I … on the other hand do so less. I fear having a better memory for the injustices and wrongs I have suffered …

In time, I found out other things like, for example, in 1937, the Izzo family was in Denmark, because Aldo's father was a distinguished professor of Italian at the University of Copenhagen. However, the Danes, who were always open to welcoming the Jews, were unfortunately unable to prevent the family from being ordered back to Italy to face Mussolini's racial laws.

From Copenhagen to Venice, life changed in an instant. Everything in Venice changes in an instant ...

> Actually, Marjorie, my father was a well-known scholar of English language and literature, and he also knew a lot about Italian literature. As an excellent humanist, he hated everything related to Mussolini and the emergence of his crude fascism. At that time,

he applied to the Ministry of Popular Culture to solicit a teaching position abroad. Teaching classes outside of Italy undoubtedly offered a golden opportunity to flee the barbarism, all the madness ... and my father, of course, didn't want to pass up such an opportunity. His reputation allowed him to secure a position at the University of Copenhagen in the Department of Italian Language and Literature. We left for Copenhagen in June of 1937. However, in September 1939, the fascist government ordered us to return to Italy for the crime of being Jewish ...

The racial laws imposed by Mussolini, an accomplice of the Reich, were as brutal as those in Nazi Germany.

As I am writing these words, I am reminded of Giorgio Bassani's novel, *The Garden of the Finzi-Continis,* and its adaptation to film by Vittorio De Sica in 1970, in which the story of two Jewish families is told; the story of a couple that lives confined in the Ferrara mansion and is later deported to Auschwitz. I think about a particular scene that could well be adapted to many other scenes in the history of my people, one of the most moving in the history of Nazi persecution: A group of Jews awaits their fate in Ferrara, a fate that for them may have been uncertain at the time, but that we know will certainly have a tragic outcome. Young people, old people, children ... no one is spared from the death, the madness, and the hatred.

Fascism and the Holocaust

The Jewish people, ancient and wise, have various ways of interpreting their history. Rabbis, poets, and historians have tried, and I, too, have modestly broached that topic, joining with other thinkers to contribute a small grain of sand to the conversation. The thread that unites my people is the thread of memory, which is persistent and tenacious.

The Shoah is considered the most tragic episode in the history of the Jewish people, who have been besieged by innumerable tragedies. During that time, an effort was made to eliminate all the Jews in Europe, and each country had its own unique way of responding. The records of Yad Vashem in Jerusalem state that seventeen percent of the Italian Jewish population died during the Shoah. While that figure is heartrending, it is important to note that a significant number of Italian Jews were saved by people—some noble, others opportunistic—who hid them. Other countries were ready to betray their Jewish populations, but Italy has not had the same antisemitic tradition as Austria and Germany, even though it lived with antisemitic legislation.

For me, my conversations with Aldo about the Shoah go back to the essential words of Primo Levi, who always wondered how that catastrophe came to be. How was such cruelty possible? And it is to those words that Aldo and I always return as though the horror still prevails today.

In the history of the Jewish people, the Holocaust, and the murder of six million Jews, continues to leave an indelible mark and permanent scars across generations. Aldo lived through that dark and cruel time in the history of humanity. He and his family hid for more than a year in the house of a high-school teacher. That was when Aldo and his brother, Alberto, decided to create a cemetery for animals. Perhaps the circumstances surrounding its origin forged the other name Aldo now uses for the Beit Chaim cemetery he cares for: The House of Life.

In order to read these memories of water (in other words, Aldo's life), it is necessary to cross the thresholds of his existence, to visit the cemetery (the old part and the new) that he looks after with such care, and to recreate his life and the journey he took with his parents to Denmark, as well as their confinement during the Holocaust. One must also understand the value of freedom as Aldo experienced it when he worked at sea and in his return to serve his community.

> Dear Marjorie. My father, Carlo Izzo, my mother, Lia Ravenna, my brother, Alberto, and I went to Denmark in June 1937. We returned to Italy in October 1939. [...] We were hidden between September 1943 until December 31, 1944. In 1947 I left the traditional high school I had been attending and went instead to the Nautical Institute ...

Aldo speaks very little about the traumatic time of the Shoah. He doesn't deny it happened, but nor does he allow it to control his life, even though it is always inherently present. That time of fascism in Mussolini's Italy was, undoubtedly, the moment when Aldo's fervent desire to escape and to travel beyond the sadness took root. And, although the war ended at some point, the persecutions continued.

Aldo, the Voice of History and Memory

As I read Aldo's messages, I would imagine him looking out at the horizon beyond the Lido and at the stars over the Adriatic, a sea that, despite the calamity of the pandemic, looked majestic and clear. And so, as the water returns everything, as everything comes and goes, Aldo emerges from the past like one of those grand Venetian personages that history has failed to recognize.

From the first time I met Aldo Izzo I sensed that he would be the key to understanding Venice, the Venice that has buried stories, that hides the time of day and night, the city that fades away beneath the fog ushered in by the Adriatic at dawn. To speak about Aldo is to enter the heart of the old Jewish community, one of the oldest in Europe.

> *That's right, Marjorie, it is one of the oldest, but it is not the first, because, as I understand it, and of course it is noted in the annals of history, Rome had the first Jewish community and then other Jewish brothers settled in Sicily. So, those communities are much, much older that the Venetian one. Actually, there were Jews in Rome as early as 300 years before Christ ...*

Walking the streets of Venice with Aldo, in person or through his letters, is akin to discovering myriad stories, some that are familiar and others that have been hidden for years. I ask him to tell me those stories, which he does with grace, patience, and wisdom. I think that perhaps taking care of the old cemetery requires the gift of patience.

For me, Aldo is an amazing figure, a character full of humility who lives amid a Jewish community that, like all other communities, sometimes experiences frictions and disagreements. When he finally returned to that community after his many years at sea, he found that although it had diminished in size, in his heart it kept growing thanks to his enduring altruism that continues to this day. His is the voice of history in that community.

Leaves of Life and Death

As our friendship grew, our trivial and serious conversations began to change into essential talks in which, in addition to discussing our most important experiences, we broached the topic of death in all its dimensions, including the death of those Aldo cares for in the cemetery, many of whom arrived there long before he was born.

Venice represents the history of the hidden made visible, the history of personages who resemble words that once uttered aloud make thoughts ripple and then vanish like the leaves that cover the paths of the Jewish cemetery. In Beit Chaim, each leaf is a forgotten life, a memory that nevertheless is recovered thanks to the dialogue that, from this side of reality, Aldo engages in with each departed person. His words are a talisman that pulls my people's dead back from the void, from oblivion. I imagine that, for them, Aldo is a larger-than-life presence, the helmsman of a barge that bobs patiently on an ocean of uncertainty, becoming for us—the survivors displaced from other times—the spirit of this city. I am sure that Aldo is simultaneously the city of Venice and the Lido cemetery.

The lagoon sparkles off in the distance while Aldo welcomes everyone with the peace deserved by those who might live amid fog and uncertainty. I think about the old cemetery where the Venetian Jews finally found peace within the mist that dissolves bodies and blends them into the horizon and time.

The Venetian Jews

Most of the Venetian Jews arrived by way of land. They came from Spain, Turkey, Germany, and from the innumerable basins of the Mediterranean, some seeking shelter, others religious tolerance. They arrived brimming with stories and weighed down by loneliness. The non-Sephardic Jews had only a few possessions to help them survive the journey, just like today's refugees. It seems it is a pilgrimage all Jewish people have in their blood, a characteristic of our culture and our species.

As I edit this text I think about the difficulty and the infinite sadness entailed in remembering times when we have been at the mercy of extermination policies. Sometimes, perhaps out of idleness, we do not reflect on how lucky we are to live in a relatively benevolent, respectful, and—one might even say—compassionate time. Perhaps out of convenience or habit we forget to think about how the harmony we observe when we look out the window or onto the street can change in an instant.

The Hiding Place During the Shoah

In one letter I asked Aldo: *Would you tell me more about where you all were when you returned to Venice?* I know I'm pressuring him a bit because Aldo doesn't answer for some time. But then, one day, I see a new message in my inbox. It's from Aldo.

> *You know, Marjorie, you inquisitive girl …*

As I read, I think about being an inquisitive girl and I chuckle.

> *Where was I? My brother and I were very young. My teacher and her sister, two spinsters, hid us in the basement of their house. They took us in and protected us. In reality, and being frank, they saved our lives by risking theirs. That's what I remember the most. I also remember how sad I felt not being able to play with my brother. We couldn't play for years, even though playing is such a simple, normal thing …*

I imagine him pointing to the Venetian houses as he writes ...

> *Do you remember what they are like? They are low to the ground, made of thick stone, and are deep, with very few trees. There aren't a lot of places to hide and even less space to wander in these houses that are so small …*

Then I think about Aldo and his brother, Alberto, having to crawl around the house so that no one from the outside would be able to see them. Aldo returns to the hallways, rooms, and basement of that small house each time he talks about his childhood refuge. Curiously, he tells me nothing about his parents during that period. It seems there are certain topics he simply will not broach.

Although Aldo sometimes tells me Venice is a city of stones and few trees, I believe that everything in Venice radiates life, and this fact is reflected in the generosity of the inhabitants of the city. Perhaps that is why many Italian Jews were saved by the goodness of Catholics who lived here, like the teacher and her sister who hid the Izzo family.

I imagine that the teacher's house only has eyes on the inside, because nothing can be seen from the outside. Outside, shadows roam the desolate streets with their insistent, constant, and repetitive footsteps. Even though it seemed to me that while they were hidden, Aldo and his family must have embraced life and imagined better times ahead, Aldo disavows me of that notion when he talks about a future rooted in a past that never changes.

> *My dear Marjorie. Europe and the world have no shame. Europe is still not satisfied with the damage it has done to the Jews. We could start with Emperor Titus, but let's not. Think about the atrocities, the torture, the "autos-da-fé" of the so-called "Holy Inquisition" in Spain. Think about the atrocities of the pogroms. Think about the six million Jews assassinated in the Nazi death camps. No, but they are still not satisfied. First, we had killed Jesus. Deicide! Then "the race," and now Israel. If you notice, the label changes but the contents of the bottle are always the same. Why? If I were to fight with all the Christians and all the Muslims in Italy, I would be alone against so many people. It's easy, really easy, to persecute a small minority of people who are "different." Difference only bothers ignorant people. Are we different? You tell me because I don't think we are …*

Braided Questions

With Aldo, I always return to the difficult questions, the complicated ones, the profound ones, the ones that are difficult to answer; questions that deal with the incomprehensible or events no one wants to revisit.

> *Dearest Marjorie. I reread your questions. It seems to me that in everything I have written, the answers can be found between the lines … Today the cemeteries reopened, but with so many restrictions. I'm quite busy. I will return to my story as soon as possible …*

Answering these kinds of questions means bringing back traumatic events, visiting in our minds those spaces where pain and tragedy comfortably roam, places in our history where madness and hatred distort everything we take for granted: both civilization and its not-too-distant counterpart, barbarity. Places where the line between the two concepts has been well defined at times and obscure at others, where everything turns into chaos, madness, and sadness. Spaces where the dehumanization of communities reigns, where informants and saviors live together in a city that never rests, where everyone has the potential for betraying his own brother in order to survive. In short, places where horror is the constant. Aldo once wrote to me:

> *Human nature doesn't change. I believed that after the horrendous atrocities of the Second World War we would have been sated with wars. That was not the case. Think about what happened thirty years ago in Bosnia and what is happening today in Ukraine. Even Hakadosh Baruch Hu was successful with the flood …*

One day when I ask him again why he decided to become the caretaker of the cemetery, he responds as follows:

My dear Marjorie, I have lived my whole life in the Lido, and this is the place where [I relive] the memory of who my brother Alberto was, so it's natural that I would be the caretaker …

For many Jewish children during the Holocaust, the cemetery was the place they could go to play in peace without being persecuted. Aldo tells me that before his family had to go into hiding, it was the only place he felt both free and safe. With the passing years, and upon his return from his naval travels, he thought that he should look after the Jewish cemetery in the Lido and participate in one of the most noble responsibilities of the Jewish people: the burial of the dead. The Talmud says that this act is so noble because it expects nothing in return, as the deceased cannot return the favor.

As I write about Aldo, I return to his childhood and to the old cemetery in the Lido where he and Alberto were free and where they felt secure among the dead.

Alberto and you,
Safe in the cemetery
Where no one pursued you,
Where you played with time
And the immense silence of those who rested there.

You found a swarm of memories,
Of truncated and victorious lives,
And among the leaning tombs
With names in sepia,
Each life emerged with splendor
While your voice and Alberto's voice
Could be heard within the mist,
Beyond all memories.

You laughed and caught fireflies
In that quiet realm
Where everything was possible,
And those who slept there listened.

The Barges of Death

Now I am imagining the older part of the Lido cemetery, the one that resonates the most in my story about the Venetian Jews. I imagine it through the seasons, during the autumn when glimmers of sun reach the foliage, when golden light reveals the names inscribed over centuries on the tombstones, bringing them back to life. Slowly the sun brings those lost names back from the dead and Aldo's dream with his brother becomes a reality. On the cemetery's paths I imagine children playing—something Aldo and Alberto could not do in the house of the teacher who once saved their lives.

In the distant past, barges were used to transport the Venetian Jews to the Lido cemetery from the Ghetto, where most of them lived. I imagine the sounds of death, the footsteps around the coffins. Did the dead make that journey at sunset? Who cared for them? What happened if the Ghetto doors were closed? Who waited with the coffins? These are questions I ask myself out loud. Sometimes I share these thoughts with Aldo, and he tells me that, with the help of our miraculous God, the dead were able to travel across the great lagoon so someone could take care of them on the other side. Were they perhaps the lost angels of Venice? I think about them and how they traveled towards the land of the dead.

Yom Kippur During the Pandemic

It's the Saturday night before the days of Yom Kippur. In Venice, those days are lived in wonder and a certain diffidence because of the great solemnity of the occasion. It is the day when we forgive that God who vacillates between presence and absence like the enchanted memory of the dead and the living. The night amazes us with the clarity of the moon and its beauty. As I gaze up at it, I imagine that, at this moment, Aldo is hurrying towards the cemetery on his winged bicycle, as though delivering messages to the dead who have been there for centuries. But in Venice time isn't measured by those worn calendars that are reminiscent of old sepia-colored family photographs. Time is measured according to the most important events and happenings that are preserved with colored ribbons, and that are like shifting and uncertain lines, like the swells of the great lagoon. I ask myself what this Yom Kippur—that is happening during the confinement of the pandemic—will be like. Surely, it's a different kind of confinement than the one that affected the Venetian Jews who were persecuted and had to remain hidden. I ask Aldo how he is coping with this confinement, the present one, and he tells me "more freely than ever," because no one is persecuting him, no one is searching for him.

Sacred Holidays

On these days called the High Holidays, I think of Aldo, the caretaker of memory and the Angel of Ashes. I imagine him unfurling his bicycle's enormous wings and riding it above the Lido's sky as he makes his way to the cemetery where every day he waters the flowers that adorn the graves. Despite death, life allows us to tell stories, and I imagine Aldo approaching each tomb and telling the dead in a low voice that their names have been inscribed in the Book of Life.

This year, on the very special day of Yom Kippur, September 28, Aldo tells me that he boarded a *vaporetto* early and then walked to the now-open gates of the Ghetto. Aldo has passed before those gates many times before, sensing the wandering dead who return in our memory for these holidays and especially for the day of forgiveness, which is also the day of remembrance. During the pandemic, people prayed in one of the most beautiful synagogues in Italy and perhaps in the world, the Levantine Synagogue, which was built in the sixteenth century for and by the Sephardic Jews who came from the Balkans and the Ottoman empire (after having been expelled from Spain in 1492). It is carved in wood and has flowers and large windows that light up the interior of the temple.[4]

It seems Venice only exists when someone desires it or loves it; it is as though a painter has embellished it and then laid it bare, or a poet has written about it only to have it vanish within the ripples of its canals. Clocks stop, the city invents its own time. Suddenly, in the distance, when no one and nothing interrupts the messages of its soft light, a liturgical and solitary Shofar can be heard, a horn that emits a long wail in some lonely Venetian alley announcing the arrival of Rosh Hashanah.

The Time of the Graceful Sea

I wonder how tourists measured time before the pandemic when they could travel hurriedly around the city. Would it be with the speed of our current short attention span, which prevents us from capturing any experience beyond the immediacy of a digital photograph? Nothing in Venice should be too fleeting or too fast, except for the rhythm of the funerals

---

4 The Levantine (Sephardic) Jews had adequate wealth to build a synagogue, one that did not occupy top-floor apartments, but was a free-standing building, an enduring testament to their resolute faith and resources (*Jewish Venice*). The synagogue still stands today, allowing visitors to take in the breathtaking red and gold interior of the building. The wooden *bimah*, or pulpit, along with the carved wooden decorations that adorn the ceiling, further reinforces the permanence of the Jews who settled there over five centuries ago (Calimani, p. 134). The powerful act of wood carving was evocative of an unwavering resolve and commitment to their ideology.

that leave the Ghetto at dawn. After the nocturnal rest that escorts bodies into that other realm, the memory of days becomes intermittent in this city, just like the tides that bring forth aromas each morning, especially after Yom Kippur when Hashem, thanks to his covenant, inscribes us in the Book of Life. Then Sukkot begins. It is a celebration where strangers are invited to spend seven days in a sukkah, a house with delicate walls made of branches; a house without a roof so we can be closer to the stars.

Living with Absence

In his messages during the High Holidays, Aldo talks to me about his wife for the first time. At the beginning of our correspondence, he told me that she had died a couple of years before, but nothing more. I ask him how he celebrated Sukkot during the pandemic, and he tells me that he spent it remembering his wife; that he dedicated himself only to remembering her, to thinking about her. He says that he sat out on his terrace where they used to sit together. Aldo lives with her absence every day. However, his memory connects him to the objects they shared in life, and despite the passing of time—which also makes palaces sink—those objects continue to be present like the clocks on St. Mark's Square chiming the hours to come. Outside, day and night bridge all the seasons. The tide rises and falls as many times as the number of different languages spoken in that city close to a moon that illuminates palaces and their silver domes.

Now in his nineties, Aldo enjoys his life amid the memories of his past when he celebrated all the Jewish holidays with family and friends. These days, he sits on his grand balcony facing the Lido and remembers. In the art of remembering, his mind produces images, which is another way of experiencing the city of Venice. As he observes the lagoon, he tells me that sometimes he thinks about and remembers his adolescence:

*It was a pretty chaste time, very different from the one in which
we now live. Perhaps a kiss on the vaporetto or an embrace when
saying goodbye to your sweetheart ...*

And then he tells me about his first encounter with his wife:

*After the War, many refugees from the Italian colonies in Eastern
Africa and many refugees from Istria and Dalmatia (territories that
the Allies took from Italy and gave to Yugoslavia) came to live here
in the Lido. Among them, of course, were boys and girls ... There
was a young girl of fourteen-and-a-half. I was eighteen-and-a-half. It
was the 21st of March 1949. Between us a very chaste love story
developed, as was the custom in those days. Then I left to work at
sea, and we fell out of touch ... You ask why I chose to work at sea
back then? As I said before, more than a choice, it was an escape,
a pressing desire to change my life. I didn't like the Lido back
then; I didn't have friends. But the main reason was the abysmal
difference in mentality and behavior between my fellow high-school
students and me. First, they were still nostalgic for Nazi-fascism, and
I, of course, was not. Perhaps also because the Lido is a small island
and I wanted to escape, to see the world. Years later, in October of
1956, we got together again. I was twenty-six and she was twenty-
two. The 10th of February 1958, we got married ...*

Then for decades Aldo and his wife celebrated Sukkots with friends who
they invited to lunch and dinner. Perhaps it is true that there were happier
times in those days.

*My dearest Marjorie. Yesterday was Shabbat and also the first day
of Sukkot, but unfortunately Venice has been experiencing high tides,
and I was unable to get to the Temple. I stayed here to reminisce
about the thirty-three years my wife and I celebrated on our terrace
in a pretty sukkah covered with a roof made of laurel branches.*

Each day we invited six people, also at midday on Shemini Atzeret.
We did that for the last time in 2014. In 2015 my wife was gravely
ill. In 2016 she died. After that I didn't do it again. Do you know
what I do now? I take the table to the place where we used to erect
our sukkah and I eat outside. Alone. Like those who pray at the Kotel,
the Wall, because at one time the Temple was there …

Sukkot
It is important to experience the uncertainty of things,
The perpetual ambiguities of days.
That's why we celebrate Sukkot
And we live for seven days in a roofless house
In order to see the stars,
In order to feel the fragile vulnerability of things,
In order to gaze at the sky and understand the invisible,
To imagine the time of goodness on Earth,
To understand yearning and the abyss.

Helena Jesurum, a dear friend of Aldo's, wrote the following to me
recently regarding her and her husband's relationship with Aldo and his
wife and the time they used to spend together during Sukkot:

In 1998, Napoleone Jesurum, who had by then become a well-
known manager in Milan, decided to return to his beloved native city
of Venice, where he was born in May 1929. He wanted to go back
to his roots. He was longing to see his Synagogue Spagnola again,
where in April 5702, 1942, he celebrated his Bar Mitzvah with
the Rabbi Ottolenghi—who was to be killed in Auschwitz. Despite
the fact that Napoleone, called "Leo" by his friends, had lived in
Milan for many years, he was welcomed with joy by his Venetian
childhood friends. A year later, Leo was appointed General Secretary
of the Jewish Community of Venice. At the same time Aldo Izzo was
responsible for the Jewish cemetery (1386—still in use) and for

this reason he also had the supervision of this ancient place. It was only too natural that Leo and Aldo, former senior naval officer and master and commander of large ships, would meet. A very sincere and genuine relationship was immediately established and from the beginning both appreciated each other profoundly. In addition, Aldo was responsible for public relations and thus gave life to a constructive and perfect collaboration and understanding with Leo. Every year for the Feast of Sukkot, Leo and I used to be invited by Aldo and his dear wife Antonietta, who we all loved deeply, to the beautiful terrace in their house at the Lido of Venice. There, we spent a wonderful time together with other friends from the community. I am delighted to say that we became real and close friends ... A memory that will last forever.

The Slow Days of the Pandemic

I am writing about Aldo during the time of the pandemic when I can only travel in my imagination. This pandemic is not the same as the scourges recounted in history books. It is not the bubonic plague that we remember as being so far removed from us. This plague intrudes upon the typical movements of humanity. It spreads throughout the world through travel, and nothing, absolutely nothing, can hide from it, because it is the master of our existence. It seems we are condemned to live with it.

I think about Aldo so far away, but at the same time somehow nearby. He tells me that the days pass as though one runs into the next, as though the pages of the calendar fall atop one another in a heap. They pile up like old tombs in some Jewish cemetery in Europe, which seems—at this moment—to be taking a break from barbarity. All the while, Aldo Izzo brings to life the memory of others, of those who were in Venice, in that city where death appears to be reflected in every brick, at every turn.

Imagined Times During the Confinement

My conversations with Aldo make me think once more about the city of water where I enjoy the feel of the falling rain, because it always seems as though the Adriatic is receding, retreating into itself, as though it is shrinking. I hear the Venetians on their way home exclaim *Signore! Signore!* as they make their way through the crowds, crossing streets that don't resemble any others in the world. And so, everything in this city vanishes behind the rain as though Venice is launching itself into an abyss of fog. As this is happening in my mind, I remember that Aldo is still looking after the cemetery. How I would love to be able to return to Venice and knock on the gates of the old cemetery, to accompany Aldo as he greets the dead. I want to imagine new stories in that city—both the old and the new—where everything seems to be a symbol or a question.

In every season Venice shines with the beauty of its old palaces where perhaps some spirit cared for by Aldo perches on high gazing at the canals. I open the sepia-colored curtains and the city looks out onto the world. Venice with its magical waters appears to be a dream that encompasses all the world's beauty. And I reflect that we, as science tells us, are also made of water, of calm waters along with other noble elements in a world that begins with birth and ends with death.

The Illusion of Autumns

When Venice begins to cloak itself in autumn, it is not only sculpted by the water but is also awash in dry leaves. The cats that during the summer announced warm nights with their pleasant mews, are now hiding. Autumn is a slow and fleeting season, as though it is preparing itself for a damp and foggy winter. The leaves fall from the trees in due course and one can feel the passage of time in a harmony that is complete. The calendar of days is shorter and lighter. The tops of the golden trees have already departed leaving only branches that paint a certain story in the darkness, a certain character or ghost that roams the empty neighborhoods inhabited now by the sound of footsteps walking away. That is when words become necessary again in order to describe in some delicate written line the phenomenon of autumn in this city ...

THE GUARDIAN OF MEMORY: ALDO IZZO

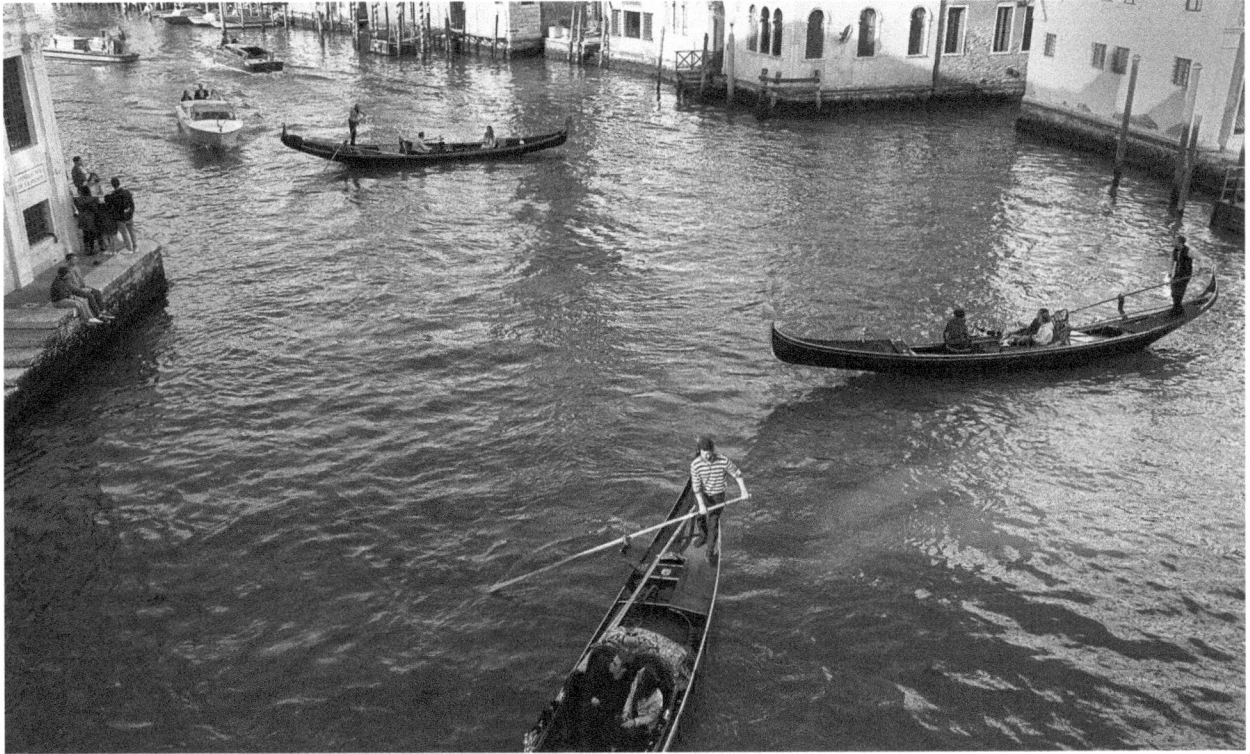

A stubborn leaf still lives amid the bare branches. Each leaf is a passing day. I pick one up to give to whomever happens close by. I want to gather all the leaves in the Lido cemetery and make a bed of them, a place of rest for the living and the dead who remain prone in that temporary season, and who, like all of us, are passengers in transit between a life and a death. In the meantime, I caress this leaf that heralds the arrival of the gray and the blue, that will keep me company and not abandon me. I will age with it until one day I will be a solitary leaf in the heart of a forest without trees, the sacred forest of memory where Aldo and I live together on that blue line between light and shadow.

Always Returning to the Lido

In my imagination, I decide to take the *vaporetto* once more to the last stop. I have made this trip so many times in my mind, but I always come across alleys that are different from those I encountered the day before, as though they change according to my experience, with the magic that is peculiar to this city that seems to want me to guess the message it is trying to convey to me in its transformations. Always in Venice, everything can change in an instant.

It is raining copiously, and the old palaces seem to play within the fog. I like to see all this up close, because through the haze everything seems a bit strange, mysterious, or even primeval. In the mist, shapes seem to ripple on the great canal, and I feel like everything I am seeing is both the reality of the here and now of a Venice that is sinking and is besieged by tourists, and a Venice that only exists in the imagination and in the love with which one admires it.

That is what I am thinking about as the *vaporetto* bobs along in the rain, and the cold merges with the wind and ruffles my skirt while umbrella vendors marvel at the long line of tourists awaiting their turn to board.

A Visit to the Dead

Suddenly a cyclone arrives off the Adriatic dissipating the ubiquitous fog, and we enter a different Venice, a Venice that can only be captured in poetry. I finally arrive at the cemetery. Larks and doves are engraved on its iron gates. Upon entering, I feel the strange peacefulness of death; the tranquility of the dead who appear to want to tell me something, some secret by way of silence or the distant mews of the cats that welcome me. Death moves us to write about its mysterious nature.

In my imagination, I have witnessed the city's barges pass by with their dead. I have seen how the canals open and let the city's shadows and water forge the paths along which we, the living, travel. Perhaps all of Venice is a path or a canal into which our lives inevitably decant. I have seen its comings and goings, its journeys between the shadows and the light, and that is what I think Aldo does every day. He comes and he goes, he cares for the dead and welcomes their families. And it seems that in those instants when the doors of life and death are opened, Venice turns into all the cities of the world. Venice and its wayward clarity, the source of all light and darkness, is sometimes a sad storm or sometimes a tear that merges with the rain. It is a story and a tremor of light.

The Silence of Permanence

During the pandemic, I imagined Aldo in the Lido where the fog and the mist made it impossible for the *vaporetti* to arrive. No horns sounded in the fog. The Lido became an island of splendor where everything bloomed again, where neighbors, both dead and alive, learned to greet one another anew. Venice in its game of absences, the city of dreams, the city of love, the city of pain. The few times Aldo went out, it must have been to bury those who had recently passed away.

The Ghetto was empty like in the Second World War when so many people were deported while others hid. The latter were the fortunate ones, but I still sense their spirits arriving on the plaza, conversing, and belonging.

I imagine once more that it is raining heavily in the city. I try to remember what I can't see with my naked eye. I try to recover each instant in Venice, and it seems to me an awesome task in the back and forth between what is and is not at the same time. And, in my memory, I head towards the Lido cemetery again, to the old tombs and the more recent ones, but I see few Venetian Jewish brothers. Are there only 500 today? Everything's a bit uncertain in this city with its inconsistent information, dates, and statistics. Finally, people come and go like tiny ghosts crossing the canals. I watch them as they wander, and I sense that the living await the dead, and the dead await the living. I join them while I recite the poem, "So as Not to Forget" by Gertrud Kolmar, who was murdered in Auschwitz, but who nevertheless accompanies us on this brief journey:

> *Night comes and I dive into the stars*
> *So as not to forget in my soul the way home.*

Venice and Love

Once you get to know Venice, it's impossible not to love it and surrender to its charms. Loving Venice is akin to longing for another person between absences and presences. This city is a constant coming and going between the past and its future while the present remains always in waiting, mysteriously submerged in order to later emerge as a new life.

Even though I do not live in Venice, I feel connected to that city where at night it seems to envelop us in the suggestive rhythm of its gaze. And so, sometimes I encounter it in the periphery of my dreams when it rises with the tide, and a siren announces something imminent, or in the presence of its *acqua alta* that carries us on its gentle ripples towards the solitude of its sea.

As I have already said, Venice is—for me—the Lido and the presence of Aldo, always ready to welcome the dead without question and without asking for anything in return, like someone who answers only to the grandeur of this city; a grandeur that reverberates in its every brick. Venice is also the Ghetto with its gates that were closed at sunset as though trying to confine and subdue an untamed sea in a futile effort to render it still, immutable. However, I believe that once the gates were shut, the Ghetto within blossomed just as spring blooms in the memory of those who undertake the journey towards death.

Venice is also what is not said and what is said without speaking, what is hidden but is always latent in the deepest part of the city that becomes the deepest part of ourselves. There, nothing is lacking if we allow our senses to swim in its canals, if we let our senses emerge in that city of relics that dazzles us as we roam through the ruins of its history. Venice is that indefinite entity that inhabits memories, that indescribable presence in dreams about an impossible city. Perhaps that is why it is remembered by those who, in writing, have tried to portray its architecture in words that at first seem to surrender to its beauty, but later manage to express it.

Venice and Its Foliage

Venice doesn't have a lot of trees, but I nevertheless feel that it's a green city with foliage that also resides in the depths of the water. I relish seeing the changing colors of the Adriatic, a mysterious milieu with its greens and aquamarines. It is a city as disquieting as that faint light that resists the piercing of the tides and oblivion, like a sea that, unannounced, assumes the splendor of an ancient history in which both death and life are woven together in a single gaze.

> *Five Glimpses from Venice*
> The sun dawned in your gaze.
> I awoke and approached the water
> To chance upon its paths.
> Beyond the early hour,
> Venice swaying, clear and radiant.

The snow has arrived on the water
Of a Venice sleeping between the sky and the sea.
The snow is opaline, is memory …
We sense the strides of shrouded footsteps,
The city is a blue mask.
Snow falls on a slumbering Venice.
The weather welcomes the memory of the snow,
The flakes like wayward stars …
And suddenly it is our own footsteps
That wake us in this city of memory,
City that brings snow from other worlds.

Nothing here obscures the soul …
Night and day in a woven thread of gold.
The sky has no shadows,
Neither does the water.
The light cascades like a waterfall,
Like pure laughter on every face.
We have followed the invisible maps of the city.
Our faces too are invisible maps,
Furrows, cities, and rivers …
Suddenly a bird alerts me to the orchestras in the sky,
The bells in ancient palaces,
Venice in our memory sheltering sounds.

Although I am leaving my imaginary Venice with these words, I don't think it's a final goodbye, because no one really bids farewell to that city forever. Its people and its strange geography mysteriously find us without us searching for them, like individuals who recognize one another in the depth of a dream or in the reappearance of that sea that I now observe in other places.

And then I choose to lose myself. To lose myself in the currents of this fragile piece of writing that is hazy at times like the sea that advances towards Venice, like the water that protects its entryways.

Returns

In 2021 when the Covid restrictions were finally relaxed, I could once again think about traveling and visiting loved ones. The first trip I planned, after visiting my family in Chile, was to Venice to see Aldo again and to visit the city that always speaks to my soul. I was excited to return and to experience the unique and mysterious rhythms of Venice and to spend time with Aldo in his home.

When I wrote to him after my first trip back to Chile in over a year, I learned something important about Aldo. Although he loves his cherished Venice, he told me:

> By the beautiful and poetic things that you write to me, I understand
> that when you return to the US you will feel nostalgic for the land of
> your childhood and your beloved Pacific Ocean … I understand why
> it makes you sad to leave your beloved Chile. I, on the other hand,
> don't feel particularly attached to any one country, I feel stateless,
> very much a "citizen of the world," in the true sense of the word …

Aldo's soul is not confined to one place, but rather extends throughout the world, and his humanity touches everyone fortunate enough to meet him.

I arrived in Venice in April of 2022 with several goals: to get to know my friend, Aldo, better; to visit the Jewish cemetery in the Lido again; to travel around Venice and see it with different eyes; and, to learn more about the rich history of the Ghetto. Aldo was also looking forward to my visit because he yearned to see his story in print. Before my trip he responded to one of my messages in which I had told him about the presentation of one of my books in Santiago.

> I'm so happy to hear about the wonderful launch of your book.
> Brava, Marjorie! Will the day come when the book you wrote about
> your Aldo Izzo will also be published? I really hope so …

And in another message, he told me:

I continue my same routine: Temple, the cemetery, back and forth, up
and down the Lido on my red bicycle … I await you in Venice with
impatience and love … You'll also have to tell me all about the book!

The Sounds of Venice

The city where Aldo lives and cares for the dead like a guardian angel welcomed me back with its unique sounds and its magical light. The sounds in Venice are also tied to the paths of the water. They appear and then fade away. They are restless and sometimes are a haven for peace. You must listen to them. Once you do hear them, you realize they are the sounds of all times. They are also the sounds of the dead keening from within the cracks of the city and its stones that speak, recount, and feel the pain of time.

As I wake anew in Venice, the first thing I hear is the water. It has been here forever like the stars and the sea. Venice, the improbable city, is full of sounds that convey a unique cartography. Sometimes when I awake, I want to travel the path of its sounds, the sounds of the day, of the Rialto Market where the fish invite us to witness the allures of the sea. The sounds also have their own gaze. It is necessary to find the voice in that gaze, to allow yourself to be carried away by the unknown, and to lose yourself in the sounds of Venice and the company of your own footsteps.

The sounds of the Lido, one of the last islands, are the sounds of where the sea and the forest meet, and beyond the Lido is the Jewish cemetery. In my mind, I walk through both the old and the new sections and I do not stop. I only listen to the sounds of silence and death. These sounds simply invite me to be present … I walk step by step and I listen step by step. I stop and I do not stop. Nothing is pursuing me, only the origin of lived dreams that I will find in each tomb; tombs that sound like rivers, estuaries, the voice of water that nothing can interrupt; the voice that always is, like life itself.

The Time of the Path
We begin to discover the time of the path
That appears and forks,
That guides us to the time of water …

We have been listening to the path's stories,
Like those that women with clay baskets sing,
Like the warps of silence
Or the clear rumble of the leaves,
Without a compass,
Without haste.

The path teaches us the impromptu time of things:
What is and is not,
Swift words that lose themselves in abysses and deafness,
Words woven in threads of gold …

And so, we become both fragile and wise,
We rescue humility in all its glory,
And without knowing where we are heading,
We arrive with the certainty of the ineffable,
With gratitude for a mysterious design.

The Imagined City

In Venice one must play with absence because it is an illusory city. We are looking at what it was, perceiving it in the past, and thinking about it in the here and now as we discover it by way of its footsteps, its sounds, its triumphant vulnerability. Venice is a woman who is cherished, assailed, conquered, but always loved, and she is always herself before us. The improbable city that speaks in its water's cadences, that loves silence, and the solitude of silence as one might love a heart in pain. At night the palaces crack open. Fallen angels appear, voices from other times, and we cannot help but fall in love with the dead, with those who lived there and who lean out to welcome us from that ineffable place of absence, of what is not, but that we intuit, nonetheless.

THE GUARDIAN OF MEMORY: ALDO IZZO

The Opaline Light

The light in Venice is opaline. It ripples and plays with the time of the water, a different time, not our time. The water's time is measured by the beauty of a graceful floating light. The time of the water teaches us to stop, to feel, to touch. The opaline light is audacious; it invites us to look ...

> **The Clear Light**
> Before, remember,
> We talked about forgotten things,
> Things we left behind in the city of water,
> Because we would return to them,
> To the clear light
> Where there was no betrayal or need for flight,
> Only the light safeguarding days and nights,
> A clear and sonorous light
> That belonged to us all,
> A light that guided us without controlling us.
> It was the light of God and the stars,
> The clear light,
> The light that escorted us
> Across the threshold between day and night.

Footsteps

Venice is a city resonant with footsteps, the footsteps of women at night in their velvet heels. Nobody wonders where they are going as they glide through the Venetian nights, enigmatic nights, nights that always dazzle, even in the darkness. The footsteps of those who are going to meet a loved one defy the realm of speed. They soar over bridges so they can finally feel they have arrived. But perhaps no one ever arrives in Venice. Perhaps Venice is not a destination, but rather a chimera, an illusion etched between wakefulness and sleep ...

The Fog in Venice
The fog in Venice captures souls and footsteps
In an endless darkness.
No step is safe ...
It's impossible to say
If we're gliding through air
Or through water.

The fog marks heartbeats.
The fog shrouds us in oblivion.
Could these be our footsteps?
Could they be abysses?
Descents into the void?

The fog in Venice has footsteps ...
It rises and falls,
It disperses in the mist.
We move closer to it.
We are not certain we'll find the lost path ...
Certainty dwells in this uncertain promenade,
In our small stumbles,
Where nothing and everything belongs to us,
Where everything seems to be a sign,
A story,
Or a great void.

Tonight, my footsteps are guiding me towards the Ghetto. Aldo had written the following about that place filled with pain, happiness, confinement, and freedom:

> The foundation of our Ghetto, as everyone knows, dates back to
> March 29, 1516. It is not the best page in the glorious history of
> the Venetian Republic, that of imprisoning Jews before the pope in
> Rome ... Before the War, the Ghetto was inhabited almost entirely

by Jews. Today there are no longer Jews in the Ghetto. Obviously the five synagogues remain, as do the community offices, two kosher restaurants, a kosher hotel, Jewish stores, the rabbi's house, the morgue, the Jewish Museum, Jewish associations, matzo bakeries (only during Passover), the mikvah, our community social center, etc. Today, all our religious, cultural, and touristic activities take place in the Ghetto ...[5]

I imagine the past when the Ghetto was inhabited only by Jewish people.[6] In the mornings the gates would be opened ... I feel the first glimmers of sunshine, the gifts of the Adriatic that has just awoken. It yawns and prepares for its comings and goings, its unpredictable tides. The Jews in the Ghetto leave for their jobs. Perhaps they felt like all the other people in this city who worked and practiced vocations. They were doctors, merchants, and master builders. I imagine them leaving in a hurry and then I imagine them returning at sunset when the Adriatic takes its leave to begin its long blue slumber.

The Ghetto at Nightfall

It was at night that the confinement in the Ghetto became apparent, when a dim light traveled through the low stone houses. It was then that the true crafts of the Jewish people began to emerge. Although the Jews were segregated and confined behind the Ghetto's walls, they managed

---

5 Prior to the presence of the Jewish Ghetto, the insubstantial parcel of land was occupied by a copper foundry, therefore deriving the name from the Italian word *gettare*, the pouring or casting of metals (Duneier, p. 6).

6 The diaspora of Jews living in the Ghetto underscores the beauty of ethnic pluralism, in addition to the power of cross-cultural dialogues and collective identities. Levantines and Ashkenazim Jews inhabited the area, alongside both Spanish and Italian Jews, together enduring the challenges of human history, as their sacred texts and traditions superseded external animosities and inherent differences.

THE GHETTO AT NIGHTFALL

to create their own community in which poetry and letters flourished. Between the hours of wakefulness and dreams they created books, poems, and other brilliant manuscripts. The Ghetto was most awake at night. The stars watched over it and continue to do so today.

In that confined space, by candlelight, the Jews found ways to rejoice and not always feel like "Others." The Ghetto, at night, turned into a mini-city as vibrant as any other city in the world, and perhaps even more so, because it was then that the residents had the opportunity to study and pray. And with the invention of coffee in sixteenth-century Europe, the nights of reflection and creativity grew longer still. A palpable current of creativity prevailed in the Ghetto every night. People wrote, prayed, cooked, and sang in Ladino, Italian, Yiddish, and sometimes in Spanish. In short, for the Jews during the Renaissance, the Ghetto became a symbolic space where a new understanding of the essence of being Jewish developed. Within the walls they perfected a sense of both belonging and not belonging in a city in which they were always subject to restrictions imposed on them by the authorities.[7]

The Ghetto listens to us and speaks to us. It tells us stories we might ordinarily overlook, and once we move away from its embrace, we realize that we have been forever changed. We discover that our imaginations and our identities remain within its walls; walls that no longer confine us, but rather represent the historical context in which the Jewish people could reimagine themselves. In the Ghetto one can feel how this unique,

---

7 The Jewish Ghetto, and the notion of a ghetto itself is inherently paradoxical, as scholars have come to recognize. The Ghetto separated the Jewish people from their Venetian counterparts, while this isolation cultivated a unique sense of identity and the eventual ability to flourish (Schwartz, p. 46). Over time, both the name and the foundation of the Venetian Ghetto were cemented, with the terminology and purpose outlasting the presence of this particular ghetto.

THE GUARDIAN OF MEMORY: ALDO IZZO

intimate life reveals itself in the gait of the elderly and the songs of children playing on the semi-paved plaza.

The Essence of Creativity and Confinement

As I walk through the Ghetto, I imagine Sara Copia Sullam once more preparing her grand salon where readings and perhaps plays took place. I see her coming and going through the illuminated streets with a compelling expression on her face that has yet to be fully understood. The night weaves together Sara's verses. Every word conjures stories, premonitions from nights of confinement in which freedom nevertheless prevailed. Nothing disturbed the Ghetto's inhabitants, only the light of dawn and the light of dusk when poets took out their watercolor paints and embroidered hope with words.

To come in contact with the Ghetto is to experience creativity, faith, bravery, prayers, and that enigmatic in-between time. It is like experiencing a time that lives within other times, where everything coalesces and flows, where the image of Sara reciting her poems accompanied by a single lyre emerges time and time again. Her poems describe men who appear as angels flying over the synagogues that are a heartrending red, that sacred and beautiful red of bricks and twilight, the red of the city of Venice.

I walk away from the Ghetto in step with many others who live in my memory and who have accompanied me on this trip. As I cross through its gates, I feel the night and the trees with the shadows they project. I also feel the rays of the moon and I remember the sound of the small stones I picked up in the cemetery where the dead awaited me in silence. The dead remember the story of their people with its forked paths and its fractured time; a story in which one can perceive the tenuous continuity of life, awakening, longing, feeling, and being.

The Nocturnal Library
Suddenly, you look out into the night
Where everything awaits ….
You open the portal of the sky
That heralds each new tomorrow,
You listen to the sounds of nightfall.
In the distance, the wind, the messenger of secrets
That reveal themselves like a fragrance
In the forest that encircles your waist.
An oboe sings in the night of books,
Its sounds blanket all sadness
And the origins of night.

You peer out at the approaching night,
And in the clear starkness of your gaze
You spritz yourself with perfume to await its arrival.
Night entails waiting, caressing, and longing,
All of which emanate from the blue threshold,
And you slip into the night as though in a dream.
Everything at night is words.
The night is a dictionary of stars.

How do books slumber at twilight?
Do they seek refuge in nocturnal libraries?
And in the silence of clocks
That fall asleep at midnight?
Do the books become accustomed
To one another,
Sheltering their blue ink,
Their torn pages,
Their alphabets of hope?

Do they dream the dreams of other books,
Like sometimes we dream the dreams of others?
Do they throb when one page falls in love with another?
And do they pretend to hold hands in the nocturnal library
When one word kisses another?

The nocturnal library sings stories.
It is built in harmony with love.
Each word adapts to the breathing of the other.
They arrive at the lighthouse of the night
Where everything awaits,
Where everything is in a clear and opaline repose,
Where pages rest,
And the heartbeat of poetry pulses more quietly.
It reclines amid the shadows of sleep,
It touches the beating heart of the world
With a verse and in silence.

The nocturnal library
Where there are no fears and there is no haste.

On this night that is different from all others, I hear the world unfurl before me while the echo of my footsteps betrays my presence. I am an observer who has come to interrupt the memory of those who passed through these same streets and who are no longer here.

The Ghetto During the Shoah

It is impossible to go to the Ghetto and not reflect on the fact that, in the middle of the twentieth century, a country as cultured as Germany dominated almost all of Europe and, with the help of Mussolini, deported countless Italian Jews.

I stop on the square to remember those who were deported from the Ghetto during the Shoah. There's a plaque here now to remember those individuals. They left from here and from other Italian cities, never to return. But I do not want to dwell on that dark and cruel memory. I prefer to think about the privilege of being alive, the gift of being here and being able to communicate with my ancestors who prayed in the five synagogues within the Venetian Ghetto. I want to celebrate the continuity of our story in the Ghetto, to see it as one more piece of the memory of my people. It is, without a doubt, a memory of lights and shadows, of nights and eternal dawns ...

Stolpersteine, the Memory Stones
You stumble, you wonder why
You lean over to see
Why you suddenly faltered while walking
Through an unhurried time,
Through a hazy twilight that's always blue.

You lean over ...
It's a small paving stone,
Plain as the truth.
On it is a name,
The person's date of birth,
The day they were taken away ...

You must lean over further
As though asking for forgiveness
For having stumbled into
History with its tenuous warps.
You want to bow before it.
You know you should kiss the stone
As when you were a girl,
You kissed the threads of the Torah.

You know about truncated lives, burned towns,
Synagogues that continue to weep
Amid the scorched smoke
Of a broken life,
A stolen life.

This stone recounts scraps of memory.
She was like you, a young seeker of dreams.
She loved Sundays in Venice,
She whistled while she walked,
She thought about the warm breeze of love,
Of first love, it would seem.
She wasn't old enough
To dress as a bride in blue,
Like Chagall's brides.
She smiled at her neighbors who denounced her
In the abyss of betrayals …

A life, like six million others,
European Jews,
Romani,
Homosexuals,
The mentally ill
In the Venetian sanatorium
Where you found her,
Her name,
And you know her life
Faded away,
Fell into the rubble,
Making hazy the memory
Of a truncated life.

You lean down and kiss the stone
And in that gesture of memory
The breath of life returns.

THE GUARDIAN OF MEMORY: ALDO IZZO

The Ghetto remained in silence during those horrifying and tragic times, but now it is coming back to life once more with new lives, with children playing soccer, and with a community of artists who regularly set up their stalls there.

Aldo's House

On the way to the Lido, I sense once more that it is far away, as though we are leaving Venice behind and heading towards other waters. I enjoy being on the slow *vaporetto* and hearing the melodious sound of the Italian language as each stop is announced. I know them all by heart, but I don't stop anywhere, because my mission is to get to the Lido as soon as possible to see Aldo.

I want to see his house, his room, his books, his study, although I know I will never know Aldo completely. It is impossible for one human being to know another fully because we all keep within us our own unique mysteries. For me, thinking about Aldo is rethinking the fragments that make up his life: births, journeys, guardianship, the sea, 37 years of sailing ... Aldo doesn't talk to me much about those things, but rather about his returns and the books his father gave him. One day during my visit, he asked me: "What is it that we love when we love something, Marjorie?" I think that more than love of the sea, Aldo loves memory.

Aldo's apartment is in an elegant and noble building made of durable cement. It is on the third floor. What I like most is that it is flooded with sunlight. We sit on the spacious balcony where Aldo used to spend Sukkot with his beloved wife. I feel like the history of the Jews is much like Aldo's terrace: a place of refuge, stories, and memory. After all, Venice was always open to being a place of refuge, memory, and the past, which is also the future of the past. Aldo invites that lady named memory to join him at his table.

In this house, nothing is opaque; there is only light. It is the light of the sun and the light of understanding, the signs of the past and the signs of the future, which happily coexist here. The telephone rings: someone is calling about a death or an important holiday. It is a message from a community that hardly exists anymore but was abundant in the past.

The Bed of Light

In Aldo's apartment, I see the bed where his mother gave birth to him. I also see mummified turtles and a delightfully messy library. It's an abode full of ritual objects like the menorah and the goblet used to bless the wine. The house is brimming with dictionaries, notebooks, and records with notes in which life and death converge. I wonder if the names of everyone in the Jewish community are written in those beautiful Venetian notebooks, along with where in the cemetery they will be buried.

While Aldo shows me his comfortable home, I notice again his bed that looks out at the sea. It is the color of a hazelnut and is soft to the touch. It was his parents' bed, Aldo and his wife's bed, and now it is only Aldo's bed that shelters and protects him.

He tells me that, at first, it was a bed where babies were born, but that now it is the bed of rest, of meditating about the quiet days and nights, fully aware of all the spirits that have occupied it and that visit him on nights with full and waning moons.

I caress Aldo's bed and sense the footsteps of history. During the time of horror, surely some noble neighbor looked after this bed to protect the traces of those footsteps, those voices, that should never be forgotten. In those times of silence, the bed preserved the stories it had yet to tell. Everything in Aldo's house has the voice of memory.

The Time of Objects

In Aldo's home, objects repose. A Torah from many centuries ago lays open and unfurls all its beauty on the dining room table where Antonietta, Aldo, and their children used to spend time together. The ancient, elongated letters of the Jewish calendar are still golden and contrast with the almost pale white color of the pages. There's a small hand that is always in the Torah so you do not lose your place while reading, but the Torah also tells us that if we do become lost, we can always find our way back home. I pause before the Torah and perceive an opaline light surrounding it. Perhaps it is the light of goodness, the light of Hashem—as Aldo says—or the light of understanding.

Every Friday, Aldo travels from the Lido to the synagogues in the Ghetto to read the Parashah and celebrate Shabbat. I imagine that he always returns home to the Torah that awaits him in the loneliness in

which he lives, the loneliness of not having his beloved wife there with him. But Aldo always leaves the door of his house open in order to commune with the dead who await him. That is why his home is not lonely, but rather full of memory; it is the place where the past merges with the future, where the future is the memory of the past.

A Slow Pace

We go for a walk so Aldo can show me other parts of the Lido that I had not had the occasion to see on my first visit. Walking with Aldo is like traveling along the paths of history, which is the memory of history. We stop to remember. Aldo's pace is always slow and can be compared to the wings of angels that, although sometimes tired, prepare for new

flights, new paths to walk. Aldo smiles. I take his arm, and he points out the first house where he lived with his parents in the Lido. We stop again as though in each pause we are returning to the vicissitudes of memory, to the peace found in the goodness of time where there are no obstacles, where the stones we find along the roadsides are the stones of memory. We take our time in order to contemplate everything around us.

As we walk, I look at Aldo's face, which, weathered by the sun and by life, tells so many stories. The sun always settles on his face where it has carved deep cracks. The lines on his forehead are like a grand horizon. This is Aldo's face that, despite everything, trusts the goodness of time. Each crevice is a story, the perpetual navigations of the soul.

THE GUARDIAN OF MEMORY: ALDO IZZO

Aldo's Face

Aldo's face is like an infinite presence that encompasses the sounds of the sea. When I look at it, it is as though I have crossed thresholds and bridges to encounter the nobility of a ship's captain who always sails towards the time of light. Once he told me a little about his relationship with the sea and his years as a captain:

> The sea is beautiful, the sea is brilliant and beautiful, but perhaps it is more beautiful when seen from the shore than from a ship. I must tell you that I am not nostalgic about, nor do I have regrets about, my 30+ years of sailing. Perhaps the regretful ones are those who have no memory, those who unknowingly disregard the bad things and only remember the good things. Unfortunately, I have a lot of memory and I remember everything: beauty, but also bad times, problems with the crew, great responsibilities ... But I'm sure of one thing: the sea has made me a better man. The sea is a great school for building character ...

Despite sleepless nights and life's murky journeys, Aldo's face is my port. He's everyone's port. I explore his face, I touch it and I find the brocades of memory, the peace of a story that contains all the love necessary to survive the oblivion of history. In peace and memory, everything is reborn.

This is Your Face
This is your face ...
Furrowed by the time of days,
By the uncertain time of days.

This is your face ...
The skin of the boy you were.
It has sweet and restless cracks.
Time has traveled upon your skin.

This is your face …
The eyes resemble two lost islands
The lips that used to part like a half-moon smile
Have lost the clear texture of their light
And have thinned like the days lived
And the days left to live.

This is your face …
That has shipwrecked so many times
In its delirium to save the world,
But you lost nothing by trying.
You were a triumphant dreamer.
You eschewed the dark lure of pettiness
And walked instead towards the light of what was possible.
You were audacious in your dreams.

This is your face …
It seems to have become
Even more handsome and alive
Despite its crevices,
The rivers that cross it.

This is your nose …
The lover of fragrances
Grateful for honeysuckle.

These are your ears
That love both the irascible wind
And the soft breeze over the prairies.

In it, your face contains who you were
And who you are,
Grateful for the time lived,
For the enlightened here and now,
For the improbable future of bountiful days.

This is your face …
You awake with it, grateful,
With the world in your gaze,
The window holding the world,
Laughter furrowed by victories and defeats,
Alert, windswept, beautifully aged.

After a while, we return home. Even though we follow the same path, it—and all the other paths I have traveled with Aldo—seems distinct somehow because of my friend's clear and precise memory that never ceases to astonish me. At the end of our walk, all that remains are Aldo's sighs. He says, "Everything passes, Marjorie. Everything passes. I love you with all my soul." Repeating his sentiment, I reply, "I love you with all my heart. Everything passes, Aldo."

ALDO'S FACE

Pesach in Venice

Today is a special day. It is Passover. Shining brightly, the light celebrates our special holiday and gives me the impression that today we Jews are not alone. The light is an angel that guides us. I think back to Passovers celebrated in the Ghetto. Tradition makes us happy with its recognition of our resilience in our search for belonging, with its attempts to preserve and not erase. On this Passover night, I am joyous. Beside me, Aldo blesses the wine and chants. We recognize each other in the ancestral melodies that unite us in the time of pain and sadness. Suddenly the entire house takes on the color of sacred things. We cannot escape the history we have had to endure, but I feel like even behind the closed doors of the Ghetto, we were free.

Aldo has given me a great gift. He has given me the understanding of life and death measured by the moment of birth and the moment of death. I have learned from him that everything is entwined like a delicate golden thread. He and I will always be soulmates because the golden threads of our memories, of our love of the Jewish people, are eternally braided together to form part of the great history that must continue to be told so that no one forgets, so that all who suffered and continue to suffer may be remembered daily in our thoughts and prayers.

> *Pesach*
> In the treeless city
> Springtime arrived
> By way of the moving water.
> Venice was a rose and a jasmine.
> Pesach also arrived
> With its wisdom, its songs,
> And I remembered that phrase that said:
> *We were all once slaves in Egypt.*

At dawn, I walk without haste
To the Venetian Ghetto.
I approach the Levantine Synagogue
Where Torahs from other centuries await me.
The synagogue is devoid of people,
But not stories.
A dove coos and sings between the large windows …

A few men arrive to pray.
A few women arrive
And sit in the back pews.
The many from the past
And the scarce few from today arrive,
Those who lived in the confinement of the Ghetto
And those who lived in freedom.
We sit separated by a perpetual history
That only flows and circulates
Like the lights in this perpetual city.

I approach the Torah, I kiss it.
It is the kiss of survival,
The kiss of history.

The House of Memory

Aldo is the embodiment of memory. Memory always returns to the past, to that which no longer exists, and to the territory of death that is out of reach but is the greatest truth we all fear. Recently, after the death of a dear friend of mine, I asked Aldo what he thinks happens after death. He replied:

What comes after death? I don't know. I look with the same
astonishment at those who say that after death there will another
life and at those who say there's nothing after death …

Sometimes I wonder if the lights in the palaces here are illuminated to defy the arrival of death so it cannot find anyone in Venice.

Aldo is Venice for me even though he does not feel he belongs to any particular country. Once he wrote to me:

> *The fact that I do not feel particularly attached to any one country is autobiographical, and is, in my opinion, easy to explain. In 1937, 1938, 1939 (I was seven, eight, nine years old). It was an impressionable age when, as you know, I was in Copenhagen, Denmark. Upon our return to fascist Italy, to Venice, we were received very poorly, which led me years later to escape via the sea. The inhabitants of the Lido have the typical mentality of island people. [It's] a narrow and closed-off environment, divided into small impenetrable circles, from which I feel that I am (and I am, in fact) excluded. I had idealized Denmark, but the Danes I met in the United States and other places were horrible people … another broken dream, another deception … I love Israel with all my being. My closest relatives and friends live there … I had thought about making Aliyah, but there were too many obstacles; the children didn't want to go, I had recently bought the apartment where I now live. I am a Jew without a country …*

It saddens me to hear my friend speak these words, but I understand him, like I understand all Jews who have been persecuted for so long. The Jewish people vacillate between two apparently contradictory universes: life and death. Aldo is the person who, for me, manages to reconcile those two universes simply by spreading love and by keeping his composure in his work with death. At the end of the day, he washes his hands, leaving behind the angel of death and ushering in the angel of life.

Aldo, Full of Light

Words and Light
You and I lived among words,
Between two oceans approaching each other.
We drew closer
After we visited our souls,
After we walked at large and together
Amid the geographies of a poem ...

We have gained the peculiar happiness
Of knowing each other
Without knowing each other,
The quiet intuition that the two of us
Were ghosts in wayward boats,
But I was still certain I was not wrong
When I waited for you, and you came.

Perhaps waiting was a way of disappearing,
Of erasing oneself like one erases a line of poetry,
Or a letter one never sends ...
I didn't want to disappear,
I wanted to wait for you quietly in the stillness of time,
To protect myself from the scant refinement of life.

And I awaited your words like someone thirsting for water,
To feel alive,
To feel that someone finally hears you
After living among the deaf ...

I was mistaken ...
There were no certainties,
Only the light ...
Only within the light

Resides the certainty of what is yearned for,
The certainty we imagined,
Perhaps the only one …

And don't forget when we played with words,
Those spoken and unspoken,
Those woven together like the sweet bread of Saturdays,
Those you embroidered for me in Italian
And those I gathered, looked after, braided together,
Like a garden that did not perish,
Like a necklace that grew, that rose …

How I loved the light, because you were in it,
In the night of the world, in the night of ideas,
In the radiant night that made me write
With the certainty that we were possible.

Aldo will continue to be my Venice, the one I learned to discover at his side as something as ephemeral and deep as letters, correspondences, that come and go, that flutter between days and weeks, months, and nights when I too have dreamed of sounds and silence. Perhaps that silence is the fear of death? Or could it be the fear of a plentiful life?

Aldo Izzo is an inexhaustible source of mystery. His gaze contains every body of water. He chose to be a sailor, and it is in the art of sailing that he returns to beloved places as well as the mystery found in the depths of the sea, which perhaps is death or perhaps is life. Aldo Izzo says he knows nothing about human nature, but it is important to note that only wise people claim ignorance.

I explore Venice and I explore myself. I am an infinite torrent of dreams and contradictions, of distant questions and non-existent answers. But Aldo Izzo is always preeminent in my thoughts and feelings. I experience and learn through his actions and can imagine everything, because imagining is living and remembering.

As I bring these meditations to a close in the Hebrew year of 5783, the doors to heaven open like a beating heart above the city of Venice, like the soul that writes and listens to the silence of the water, to the day and the night, to the peace of slumbering clocks, and to the books resting in old libraries in this city that always reflects back on itself. In other words, there is renewed hope. At the beginning of 5783, Aldo wrote to me:

> I wish you and those you love a peaceful 5783. We are leaving 5782 behind us. It was the year in which we saw the beginning of the infamous and terrible war in Ukraine, which was a disaster for everyone. Will it end in 5783? Let's hope so. Hope is always the last thing to perish …

Of Arrivals and Farewells

This text, dedicated to Aldo Izzo, represents the fluid comings and goings of his life, an exceptional life that mirrors all our lives. Aldo's singularity resides in his tenacity and his persistence, in the challenges of memory, in the fulfillment of the rites of death and good deeds.

Every day, Aldo awakes determined to discharge his obligations to the dead and to participate in farewell ceremonies or ceremonies pertaining to the present: births, holy holidays, Shabbat. His is a life that has its own rhythm and calendar. His is also a life that is comprised of the unpredictable: events that no one can foretell when they will occur, like the hour of death or the hour of birth.

This compendium of texts is presented as a collection of interludes of time, of history, of the individual, and of the vicissitudes of human cruelty and goodness. Aldo Izzo's story is the story of a boy who, along with his brother, Alberto, found freedom and peace in the old Jewish cemetery in the Lido. After working at sea for more than three decades, Aldo returns and preserves the memory of his childhood; the continuous return to the Lido and to the city of those who are no longer with us.

Water, life, and death are the protagonists of these fragmentary tales. Venice is present on every page and seems close by and distant at the same time. Aldo comes and goes with the same rhythm of the sea, with his life that weaves together the story of life and death, which is everyone's story.

Within this background, Venice appears as both real and imaginary. It is a place that leaves us speechless because it is an improbable city that has managed to persist throughout the ages. One never leaves Venice; one only returns to braided time where the past and the future converge to create its present.

Like Venice, this text with its questions and answers is fluid. Its segments come and go like the swells of the Adriatic. Aldo's identity and my own identity—as the person asking the questions—are also constructed in a subtle way, as if writing becomes a mutual gaze, but at the same time an individual one in the ambiguity and fear of inserting oneself into another's life, into a measured distance.

This text is also a love letter to the coalescence of past and present, to the exploration of memory, and to the commitment to remembering. When I wrote this book, I also felt as though it was a letter made of water that would end up floating down the Adriatic where an unexpected reader would pick it up and read it, like all love letters that arrive without us expecting them ... Just as love finds us, poetry also finds us, and the indecipherable and the mysterious—like life and death—entwine. More than anything, Aldo Izzo, the guardian of memory, honors the vulnerability of time and love.

This chronicle reveals the importance of listening, of letting another tell his story, and also of glimpsing a life that perhaps had remained hidden before the act of writing. I feel very fortunate to have the opportunity to dialogue with Aldo, to get to know his motivations, his passions in a life that is in constant motion, like the sea that is adrift and has no end, just like these meditations about the guardian of memory. Aldo is also a guardian who is at times reticent and solitary, always yielding dignity to others by burying the dead who are unable to reward him for his efforts. I am writing these reflections about Aldo Izzo so that others can behold his twinkling eyes, the nobility of his hands that commemorate the circularity of time, the time of life itself.

The resplendence of literature resides in the magic of its words that alight in the minds of authors who immerse themselves in the landscape of fertile imagination. After finishing this chronicle or reflection about Aldo Izzo's life, I understand that literature is also the voice of the other. It is not only the art of narrating, but the art of encountering the voice of an interlocuter that allows you to listen deeply to what is being recounted. It is also an act of reciprocity and a delicate balance between what is said and what is left unsaid, between the finality and the endlessness of the art of storytelling.

Literature is a path towards the art of patience and beauty. Writing and reading are acts of faith. They represent the reciprocity of intersecting voices and gazes. In this work of literature, Aldo is an open poem, a violin in the solitude of the forest, a firefly that glimmers in the darkness. I invite you to enter his life as though you are entering one of Venice's canals. We will arrive without haste to his soul where goodness and memory dwell, where history nests with its splendor and its challenges. And while no life can be completely understood, Aldo's life provides infinite clues about what it means to live in order to acknowledge the passing of time and history.

Afterword to The Guardian of Memory *by Mark Bernheim*

A question: Just how does one "guard" a memory? You cannot wrap it, you cannot enclose it, you cannot keep it for one second longer than it takes for the memory to change from the present to a souvenir, a look back. Memory and dream are both more real than an unlived, unpleasant present. They take on color and substance from a palette already dried, each tint only a shadow of what it held. Dante told us how bitter it is to remember joy in a time of suffering. But at such a moment, only memory and dream can nourish, and can be expressed best in art.

Marjorie Agosín gifted her readers with *Beyond the Time of Words* earlier in 2022, an extended meditation on the power of poetry to endure at a time of greatest crisis, a worldwide epidemic which distanced millions from other millions, and those who loved most deeply from the objects of that love. Covid-19 was a challenge she grappled with like few others. In her isolation from family, from students, from colleagues, she surrendered her life-on-the-move from Chile to Massachusetts to Maine to Europe and constructed a refuge as well as an opening through language. Writing poems daily to maintain her connection to a receding world, she overcame as few others the despair of enclosure and reduction. Others could not hear her words first-hand, so she preserved her thoughts and emotions in a softly tumbling chorus of poetry. When life seemed most fragile, she found in language the means to move past words into a time reborn where all was at stake, the enormous challenge of a gifted poet to connect in time when time itself was frozen but also raced ahead into uncertainty.

Marjorie Agosín knew Aldo Izzo before Covid had kept them apart and then miraculously found him still waiting, in his tenth decade of a meaningful life, when she could return to Venice in 2022; Venice the unreal city that "exists only when one desires it, when one loves it." The plague, our plague of 2020, is both different from and the same as other plagues; for instance, the pestilence of 1348, which entered via the same waters as cholera century after century, its power to destroy immortalized by Thomas Mann in Venice. All plagues come with the same temptation to surrender life, which makes them (Covid included) deadly to our social selves. For what are we without that part of ourselves?

Marjorie Agosín in all her opus braids past and present and future as they flow within her and keep alive her precious ancestors and the legacies she carries from them. She is a woman you might meet in a Viennese Kaffeehaus, a Chilean garden, an American academic seminar, on a pebbly Maine beach, or a leafy Boston lane. She is never unaccompanied because her forbears have never left her. They fill her with their own heroic escapes and quotidian lives, their accents of central Europe, of boats crossing foreign seas, of Argentina and Chile and Georgia and New England. She encapsulates Jewish history in unexpected ways—a woman modest, even mute on her accomplishments, a woman above all with fierce weapons in words and images, a woman emboldened above men, a woman who finds her place in Jewish history above sectarian divide, a Jewish core with a universal voice that recognizes the need to obliterate suffering with the joy of artistic creation and beauty.

She answered Dante's call and found ways in poetry and meditation to remember joy and beauty at a moment of total extremis, a tunnel we could not be sure had an exit at all. For her, having inspiration and guidance from the unique Aldo Izzo in Venice gave her a key she herself crafted to open a door behind which darkness seemed to envelop all.

Aldo Izzo for her is Venice in all its history and liquid purity. His guardianship of the ancient Lido cemetery where Jews lie in the quiet of the ages has shown her a radiant example of commitment, love, determination, and valor. Her poetry brings his actions to their fullest significance for they both need each other and stand alone. Venice is built on sand and water, which changes its affect minute by minute. Look from a *vaporetto* or *traghetto* at the *palazzi* and impress the beauty in your mind, then look away to tie your shoe or straighten your jacket. Now look again and what you saw before is no more, it's gone. Another impossible beauty has taken its place, another vista you want to keep forever, but fast, it's gone again as the boat chugs and turns a watery corner.

Marjorie Agosín knows the Nobel-valued poetry of another perpetual immigrant, Joseph Brodsky. Of the countless chroniclers of Venice, Brodsky may reign supreme. He visited the city every bitter winter for decades, choosing the time when fewest tourists would be there.

In "Watermark," Brodsky's oceanic hymn to Venice (where he knew he would be buried), "Time drowns in every canal." The architects of the city were magicians to Brodsky, savants who knew how to "subdue the sea to confound time," who created the greatest masterpiece, Brodsky believed, ever produced, his Eden, his taste of Paradise.

Venice's surfaces create dust, and "dust is the flesh of time." "When it comes to time, Venetians are the world's greatest experts." For Brodsky, time is water, and only the Venetians could conquer both. They tamed time, fenced it, caged it. Made bridges to the stars, subdued time to give man a chance to breathe and live.

Aldo Izzo in Marjorie Agosín's *Guardian of Memory* is her other self. They both have sailed and wandered the world, he an artist of the Jewish life of memory, she an artist of crafting the memories packed in Jewish haste and unpacked in love of all those she reveres. They reflect each other though different in all ways, but linked and sharing what if we are lucky will endure no matter what crises—and they are already with us—are yet to come. That's what Venice is all about, dear readers, the way our reflections in our lives are stored in water better than in earth. Look at Venice and each *palazzo*'s reflection, at you reflecting on it. After a second, it's gone, as we will be. But in the water we are privileged to step on, defying gravity, in that water will be stored our reflections for when we are long gone. Marjorie Agosín's poems in *Beyond the Time of Words* and here in her *Guardian of Memory* are of the quality that will endure long after our time. As Brodsky knew, "the only thing that could beat this city of water would be a city built in the air." For that we must still wait.

Mark Bernheim
Emeritus Fulbright Professor

The Photographer: Samuel Shats, Ripples in Time ... by Mark Bernheim

A melody for the piano is transformed into a symphony, notes for a solo become the movements of a concerto. Music has the possibility for this translated, reimagined, reborn life in ways that a poem in one language finds a new expression in another. The best translations somehow find another voice when even not a single word may be the same.

Photography and poetry may exist in different planes altogether, but the finest moments of verse may stop for a moment in their rush toward meaning and lend themselves to eternity in the magic box of light and dark mixed in the camera "room" of the small machine that freezes incandescence like a wave about to break on a shore.

Marjorie Agosín's odyssey with Aldo Izzo to tell the story of the Lido's ancient Jewish cemetery entrusted to the safekeeping of his devoted soul is greatly enriched by the methodically curated photographs of Samuel Shats in this book. From long experience in his native Chile, as well as decades lived in Israel, Samuel Shats joined his friend for her days and evenings in *La Serenissima*; seeing his luminous and brooding black-and-white photographic poems is an integral part of the experience.

Aldo and Marjorie gladly share their fleeting moments of ever-changing Venetian time with Samuel and his unending immeasurable palette of grays. Velvet is warm, lacquer is cold: here feel the temperatures for gun metal, battleship, smoke, haze, fog, dove, pearl, pewter, platinum, pebble, pumice, iron, slate, ash, flint, carbon, cloud, asphalt, nickel, and stone.

All these swirl through his shots of the Venetian *palazzi*, the facades, the crumbling alleyways and doorframes. Everywhere is the water in gray, sometimes rushing, sometimes immobile, but always taking in the human gaze, holding it in reflection for just an instant more than we can conceive, seeming to drown it but in fact giving it eternal substance.

Marjorie's narrative, Samuel's photos, both virtuoso, demanding our attention but humbly paying back in beauty what no other place has ever plumbed. Walk with them both freely; if there were an entry fee, the one shot of them both walking in measured steps on the Lido's actual land-based main street would repay thousand-fold.

You will not forget either of them, and Samuel Shats makes that certain with his own art.

Mark Bernheim
Emeritus Fulbright Professor

Chronology

1096: With the coming of the first crusade, significant slaughters of Jewish people took place, particularly in France and Germany, with a notable sequestration occurring in Frankfurt am Main (Duneier, p. 5).

1290: The Jewish people were expelled from England (Duneier, p. 5).

1306–94: The Jewish people were expelled from France (Duneier, p. 5). The expulsions from France and England (1290) were due in part to the lending operations built by Jews, who had power over monasteries, lords, and kings, owing innumerable debts.

1385: Though Jewish individuals were denied permanent resident permits, Jewish residents settled the region of Venice for a cost of 4,000 ducats, the collection of which was enforced by independently elected leaders (Calimani, p. 7).

1386: The Republic of Venice allowed the Jewish people to create their own cemetery on a non-cultivated section of land near San Nicolò of Lido ("Jewish cemetery").

1443: A ruling was reached proclaiming that Jewish people could not run schools of any kind. The ruling stated that Jews could not receive any Jewish-led instruction in singing and dancing (Calimani, p. 10), which was particularly egregious considering that Jews were forced to attend Christian sermons.

1496: Jewish people were required to wear a yellow hat (Calimani, p. 11), as the original patch was deemed not conspicuous enough, signaling the beginning of generations of othering and persecution through textile demarcation.

1516: Jews were restricted to residing in the Venetian Ghetto, which was enclosed by gates and guarded consistently by Christians. They were also required to pay a tax upon entry and exit (Calimani, p. 33).

1528-31: Settlement of the area, in the initial stages by the European Ashkenazim, led to the creation of religious worship sites. The erection of two synagogues, the Scuola Grande Tedesca (1528) and the Scuola Canton (1531) (Calimani, p. 133), covertly established intentionally hidden places of worship and communal gathering for the growing Jewish community.

1541: The Venetian Ghetto was permitted the chance to add an extension (Calimani, p. 46), which occurred in conjunction with the growth and success of the Levantine Jewish community. The Levantines had adequate finances and built a free-standing synagogue which housed a wooden bimah that still stands today.

1575: The poorer Ashkenazim, or Italian Jews, migrated to Venice and built a distinct synagogue in the same square as the German shul ("History and Culture"). The synagogue was located in a sacred area with a cupola (Calimani, p. 134).

1630: The plague of 1630 proved devastating to the Venetian people; 150,000 residents died (Calimani, p. 201). Jewish merchants had to suspend their import-export operations with the Turkish people, which had tremendous socioeconomic consequences.

1655: The Ghetto reached its peak population, housing over 4,000 residents (4,870 in 1655) within two-and-a-half city blocks (Calimani, p. 149).

1682: Pope Innocent XI outlawed Jewish loan-banking, which was incredibly detrimental to the Jewish people, as it undermined and effectively eliminated one of their only legal occupations (Schwartz, p. 59).

1684–99: The Jewish people withstood a costly campaign against the Turks, leading to mounting debts and ongoing financial instability in the Ghetto (Schwartz, p. 59).

1777: The Senate reaffirmed their decision to deny Jews the right to citizenship (Calimani, p. 242).

1797: Napoleon arrived with his armies (Calimani, p. 247) and subsequently ceded the city to Austria, rendering equality for Jews an afterthought, although the Venetian Jews enjoyed some new freedoms (Calimani, p. 257).

1814: Pope Paul VII sent the Jewish people back into forced segregation, triggering street protests by Roman citizens (Duneier, p. 12).

1848 and nineteenth century: Austrian troops vacated the city, resulting in the physical removal of the gates; however, Jews remained in the area until 1870. Ghettoization came to an immediate conclusion once the Papal States were dismantled (Duneier, p. 228). Italian troops abolished the Ghetto and unified the city (Duneier, p. 12), ushering in an era of equal rights for Jewish people, as supported by Venetian laws.

1938: The fascist racial laws impacted the entire Jewish community in Italy, and intermarriage between Catholics and Jews became increasingly difficult (Calimani, p. 277). There were about 1,200 Jewish residents of the Ghetto who faced overtly prejudicial practices prior to the start of the Second World War. Discrimination became widespread, causing the significant unemployment and marginalization of the Jewish people.

1943–4: In September of 1943 German troops arrived, commencing a man-hunt and roundup of Jews. Frequent deportations continued over the course of the following year (Calimani, p. 279), leading to deaths of entire families and devastation to the Venetian Ghetto community.

1999: As a result of funding from international and Italian public and private enterprises, memorials in the Lido cemetery were restored and catalogued, preserving history that can be dated back to as early as 1550 (*Jewish Museum of Venice*).

2016: 500th anniversary celebrations of the Ghetto took place, including concerts, lectures, and historical exhibitions (Worrall). The area now houses about 600 Jewish people (Calimani, p. 281) and remains the center of Jewish life in the city.

Works Cited

Calimani, Riccardo. *The Ghetto of Venice*. M. Evans & Co., 1987.

Duneier, Mitchell. *Ghetto: The Invention of a Place, The History of an Idea*. Farrar, Straus, & Giroux, 2016.

"History & Culture: The Jewish Ghetto." *Jewish Venice*. Accessed June 1, 2021. www.jewishvenice.org/history-culture/#1526539385425-280228f4-8c16.

"Jewish Cemetery on the Lido." *World Monuments Fund*. Accessed June 1, 2021. www.wmf.org/project/jewish-cemetery-lido.

Kolmar, Gertrud. *The Selected Poems of Gertrud Kolmar*, translated by Henry Smith. Seabury Press, 1975, p. 38.

Schwartz, Daniel B. *Ghetto: The History of a Word*. Harvard University Press, 2019.

Worrall, Simon. "The Centuries-Old History of Venice's Jewish Ghetto: A Look Back on the 500-year History and Intellectual Life of One of the World's Oldest Jewish Quarters." *Smithsonian Journeys Quarterly*, November 6, 2015. www.smithsonianmag.com/travel/venice-ghetto-jews-italy-anniversary-shaul-bassi-180956867/. Accessed June 1, 2021.

Acknowledgments

I would like to express my deep gratitude to Professor Murray Baumgarten for suggesting my name as a writer in residence in Beit Venezia in 2019. Shaul Bassi kindly hosted me and gave me the artistic freedom to write about the Venice ghetto.

I was fortunate to meet Aldo Izzo and without his luminous presence and his generosity, this book could not have been written. I am grateful to Helena Jesurum and Roberta Orlando for their friendship and for their beautiful companionship while I was in Venice.

My thanks to Wellesley College for a semester's leave that allowed me to work in Venice and to the Jasper Whiting Foundation for a travel fellowship in order to complete this project.

I thank Samuel Shats for his insightful photography as well as Katie Trostel for the book's foreword, Shaul Bassi for the prologue, and Mark Bernheim for the afterword. These texts have given richness to the life of Aldo Izzo. I also thank Bethany Pasko for her research on the chronology of the Venice ghetto.

I am grateful to Solis Press for their constant support of my work and for their vision and inspiration, and to Alison Ridley for her superb translation and her beautiful rendering from the Spanish to the English.

I thank my husband John Wiggins for his companionship, his love, and support of my work.

Marjorie Agosín
Andrew Mellon Professor in the Humanities
Wellesley College

Milton Keynes UK
Ingram Content Group UK Ltd.
UKHW051033100124
435744UK00004B/85

9 781910 146842